LETTERS
FROM A
WILD STATE

LETTERS
FROM A
WILD STATE

REDISCOVERING OUR TRUE
RELATIONSHIP TO NATURE

JAMES G. COWAN

BELL TOWER
New York

Published by Bell Tower, an imprint of Harmony Books,
a division of Crown Publishers, Inc.,
201 East 50th Street, New York, New York 10022.
Member of the Crown Publishing Group.

Originally published in Great Britain by Element Books Limited in 1991.

Harmony, Bell Tower, and colophon are trademarks of Crown
Publishers, Inc.

Manufactured in the United States of America
Illustrations by Martin Rieser

Library of Congress Cataloging-in-Publication Data

Cowan, James G., 1942–
    Letters from a wild state : rediscovering our true relationship to
nature / James Cowan.
        p.   cm.
    Includes index.
        1. Natural history—Australia. 2. Australian aborigines.
    I. Title.
    QH197.C68   1991
    508.94–dc20   91-40127
                                                            CIP

ISBN 0-517-58770-X
10 9 8 7 6 5 4 3 2 1
First American Edition

For Wendy

CONTENTS

Burn brilliantly, but only at your will;
and, despising every particular thing
draw power from everything.

Paul Valéry, *Monsieur Teste*

PREFACE

The French philosopher Charles Montesquieu (1689–1755) wrote in *The Persian Letters* that the whole delight in his book 'consisted in the eternal contrast between real things and the unusual, new, or strange ways in which those things are perceived'. He further concluded that all things, including so-called 'reality', are subjective and relative to time, place, climate, religious belief, racial and national prejudice and, above all, to intelligence.

This seemed to me to be an ideal premise upon which to begin a series of letters—or at least to conduct a correspondence with myself that might yield important insights into the ironies and conflicts surrounding the modern condition as we know it. To contrast the traditional perspective of nomadic Aborigines and their reliance on the Paleolithic vision against that of our own Aristotelian world-view promised a rich lode of revelations—provided, of course, I was willing to examine myself and my time with the same degree of exactitude as we have theirs. For over one hundred years now anthropologists have been studiously observing and making judgements about the lives of primitive peoples throughout the world from a position of assumed superiority. I felt it was time that any criticisms such peoples might have of us were contrasted with our own philosophic self-confidence as criteria for further discussion.

Letters from a Wild State relies also upon another, more modern dictum made by the poet William Carlos Williams. 'No ideas but in things' governed his view of the world, poetic and otherwise. It seemed a fitting point from which to begin my own journey into those visionary realms where all true sages feel at ease. For it is a fact that today we are generally more absorbed in political, economic, and sociological considerations than we are in what traditional peoples regard as essential. The metaphysical realm is *the* only reality for them. They acknowledge the earth as gorgeously real; a world in which, as the Islamic mystic and teacher Suhrawardi (1140–1190) once noted, 'exist dimensions and extension, other than the pleroma of Intelligences and other that the world governed by the Souls of the Spheres, a world with so many cities that it is almost impossible to count their number'. If we substitute landscapes for cities I believe we come close to what an Aboriginal tribesman, surrounded by the full flowering of his tradition, genuinely feels about the land he inhabits.

It struck me, therefore, that I must return, if only in my imagination, to the metaphysical terrain I had visited over the past ten years in the company of my Aboriginal friends. They had always been courteous guides, willing to share

with me their other-worldly perspective—a perspective
saturated with the exploits of world-creators like Jarapiri,
the Great Snake, the Maletji Law Dogs, those wraith-like
spirits known as the Mimi, and Mamu-boijunda, the
Spider-man, whose incarnation presaged the beginnings
of life on this earth.

I hope *Letters from a Wild State* conveys some of the joy I
experienced on these journeys in the Australian wilderness. For many of us today open spaces have become an
icon for an age increasingly hemmed in by the growth of
the industrial state. We look to the clear air and emptiness
they offer to give us sustenance—a sustenance that in the
past was supplied by traditional religious doctrines,
whether Christian or otherwise. Like it or not, wilderness
and deserts, mountain summits and nordic wastes—
wherever they might be—have become a substitute for the
temples and cathedrals of old. They allow us the opportunity to celebrate our essential unity with nature and with
what Henry Corbin termed the 'interworld'. I have tried to
explore this interworld by way of the 'eternal contrast' that
Montesquieu spoke of when he attempted to analyse the
mœurs of eighteenth-century France.

We should never forget how important the wild world
of nature is as a tonic to the soul. Religious doctrine may
give form to the great metaphors, the myths and rites that
govern our lives. It may grant us mystical insight by way
of ascetic disciplines such as those experienced by St. John
of the Cross, Maximus the Confessor or Dante. It may
even lead us along paths of spiritual enlightenment
whereby we personally attain a deeper sense of well-being,
even bliss. But it is to the earth upon which we walk that
we should occasionally look if we are to preserve our intellectual and spiritual heritage. If we destroy this because

of our insensitivity to it as a metaphysical environment, we are in danger of destroying ourselves.

This is the great lesson all traditional peoples can teach us: how to protect who we are by protecting what made us. As one old tribesman remarked to me, 'If we do not sing the songs, the animals will go away. Then we will all die'. Clearly the act of expressing the connateness between man and earth is important to the survival of all species. *Letters from a Wild State*, I hope, is about reviving the gift of song, about celebrating wild simplicities, about hanging onto what we are in danger of losing. My own belief is that we must generate a new enthusiasm for the rediscovery of the interworld—even if it means resorting to the unorthodox.

Some of these essays have appeared in *Resurgence, Temenos*, and *Avaloka*. Dr. Kathleen Raine, Satish Kumar, and Arthur Versluis, all editors and friends, have encouraged the completion of this work. And to Julia McCutchen, whose instinct for the unusual compares favourably with Montesquieu's, my thanks. Richard Dickinson, old friend and fellow-journeyer, your patience to oversee the final manuscript has not gone unnoticed. Nor has the work of the late E. T. Brandl in his remarkable reproductions of ancient cave motifs from *Australian Aboriginal Paintings in Western and Central Arnhem Land*.

James G. Cowan
Sydney

LETTERS

FROM A

WILD STATE

ONE

ON THE
WILD STATE

The earth is a paradise . . . We only have to make ourselves fit to inhabit it.

HENRY MILLER

My dear friend,

I do apologise for not writing to you earlier. But my journey here into this wild state has been long and arduous, sometimes even dangerous, and filled with moments when I was forced to question my own motives for making such an expedition in the first place. It has therefore been impossible for me until now to achieve the necessary state of equilibrium in which to address your concerns for my well-being. Had I known that crossing the frontier into this new territory would have meant so much in terms of disrupting my normal mode of thought, I suspect that I might have had second thoughts about making this journey!

The truth is that entering a wild state is fraught with risk. For people such as ourselves, who have been, shall

1

we say, long used to a certain scepticism with regard to
belief, it is often difficult to come to terms with the existence of a so-called pristine environment such as exists
out here. Nevertheless, the traditional custodians who
live in this remote region of the world are at pains to
view their land in this way. As far as I have been able to
ascertain from my discussions with them, there appears
to be a numinous agent at work within the earth itself,
which predisposes these people to regard everything
about them as sacred. You can imagine how strange I
felt initially when I was confronted with this concept of
'sacred geography'. It was as if I were encountering, for
the first time, certain illuminated manuscripts from the
Middle Ages which suggested that Jerusalem was, in
spite of all reason to the contrary, the *axis mundi* of the
world.

Yet here I am, living in the middle of what can only
be described as a fertile desert, an Eden. The waterhole
I am camped beside is filled with a wide variety of bird
life, along with one aging crocodile who eyes me with
a circumspection that one often finds among savage
beasts bent upon stalking their prey. Wild buffalo forage
in the shallows and sea eagles occasionally luff in the
warm midday airs. At night I often hear wild boar bury-
ing their snouts in the mud by the billabong as they
search for succulent roots. For the most part I live here
alone. The birds in this primeval wonderland are my
only consorts. Pelican and duck, stork and magpie geese
combine with a host of smaller birds in a singular chorus
to register their accord with my presence in their midst.
Strangely enough, they see me not as an interloper, but
as someone who is able to celebrate with them the joy at
being free.

Of course, when I originally crossed over the frontier into this wild state, I felt sure that I would be able to deal with anything that might arise. It did not occur to me that conditions here would be so very different. I was, after all, *modern*. My existence was derived from a contemporary infrastructure that sought to raise the idea of comfort to that of Holy Writ. The modern world, with its penchant for gaudy ephemera, had made me, like so many others, into one of its willing victims. I had no wish to turn my back on all this softness, all this undeniable extravagance and journey to a place where modernity was neither understood nor desired. Yet, in spite of this, here I am inhabiting a region that has not yet bartered away its pristine condition in order to gain for itself a veneer of what we call 'civilisation'.

Disturbing perhaps? Clearly, bird feathers on a bush track bear no relation to a bulging bank account. Nor is it easy to equate the rough texture of a sun-dried buffalo skull to that of those vibrant fabrics that we wind about our mannequins. There is indeed so much out here that tests my ready assumptions about what we, in our world, find *impossible to do without* in order to survive. Journeying from a modern state into this wild state has forced me to come to terms with those golden calves of philosophy that I have always believed to be the veritable pride of the herd! The very principle of economics, for example, a mode of perception to which we all so slavishly adhere, now seems devoid of any interior dimension when I compare it to the seasonal migration of birds!

A madness you think, this confusion of one discipline with another? In the modern state we are loath to equate the workings of nature with those of man. For centuries we have learnt to celebrate the ability of the mind to detach itself from the workings of nature. Cartesian skulduggery has managed to weave its magic in the form of certain concepts such as 'thought preceding existence'! But when I look into the eye of a snake, or when I stumble upon a towering anthill, perfectly aligned with magnetic north, I begin to suspect that whatever 'thought' that precedes existence out here in the wilderness draws its energy from an entirely other-worldly source. I am led to the conclusion that life in the wild state is so thoroughly divorced from any rigid categories that it resists all our attempts to define it.

Clearly, I made this journey in order to discover whether those primordial qualities one finds in a wild state might invoke in me some residue of innocence. I was looking to the infolding wings of a pelican or the morning bloom of a lotus to awaken me again to that curious wonder that one associates with childhood. You might ask: why revert to a mode of perception that has no need of relative values? Such a mode of perception precludes the value of material usefulness or *utility*. To observe as a child denies nature its potential to serve man in the way we have come to expect. And, equally, not to regard nature as subservient to our desires is to condemn ourselves to the immature yearnings of our forebears.

I recall one celebrated sage who suggested that real power comes to those who regain for themselves a state of instinctiveness. In this wild state I have noticed that all life relies in large measure on what we choose to reject. Is it not strange that nature relies so much on the workings of instinct, whether it be the bee's innate ability to hexagonalise its existence or the salmon's Odyssean swim from river to sea? Without this order, without nature's ability to reproduce immemorial patterns, I suspect anarchy would be the norm of existence rather than an aberration.

I have no qualms about making such statements now that I have learnt to identify with nature. For once we are in collusion. I stand on the edge of this vast swampland, where the crocodile's inordinate hunger is as regenerative in its own way as the fructive gesture of the monsoon rains, and ask myself why it should be so. How is it a crocodile can drag a kangaroo from the bank, crush it to death in its monstrous jaws, and yet find itself contributing to the regenerative process as much as do the seasonal rains? Death and rebirth are forever locked in the jaws of this primeval carnivore, a fragile *conjunctio* that nevertheless holds all mysteries within its grasp.

You see, I have begun to recognise that we moderns have lost all sense of what is sacred. The nomads of this region assure me the earthly envelope in which I find myself is one vast and tremulous icon. Morning dew on a spider's web clings to a form that merely echoes each mandala about the head of a Byzantine saint. See! All nature somehow celebrates sanctity by way of an inner meaning that transcends even the symbol itself. I am constantly amazed by the easy mosaic made by leaves bent upon decorating those patient circles within wood that few of us are ever privileged to witness. It is this *substance*, I suppose, that is so visible in the wild state. For at each moment we are being confronted by the endless nurturing of the forms of nature, the perfect delineations of what is clearly inexpressible by way of rational thought.

So, you may say, my friend has reverted back to a primitive condition. He wishes to give up what we moderns have gained in the interests of pursuing some ephemeral idea of innocence. Rousseau's noble savage reincarnated! His escape into a wild state has done little more than weaken our own precarious position as lords of the world. Allowing himself to become seduced by illiterate nomads who are tethered by superstition to a set of inconsistent and often bizarre beliefs makes him a prime case for the title of embittered exile. Under these circumstances you condemn me to a life of wandering, impeded once more by my own instincts, an onlooker only in man's quest for material success.

But I say to you, think again! It is not for nothing we are blessed with a pentagram of senses, the endless knot of sensations that together surround us as if they were the seductive wreath of Niniane's veil. For it was she who captivated Merlin and so imprisoned him forever in the Forest of Broceliande because of his desire to know all, to penetrate this veil. For he, like ourselves, wanted to unite with matter in his bid to achieve immortality. This heady concoction was to lead to his imprisonment, a victim of his own magic rather than the wiles of the forest sprite. She merely offered him her undying love in return for the secret of his wizardry. He, the great shaman, the hierophant, the husbandman of mysteries, now found himself disenfranchised by the illusory beauty of Niniane, the very embodiment of Maya. And I say to you that it is we who are prepared to destroy the wizardry of nature by following the way of reason and not the spirit in our bid to see through this same illusory veil.

The custodians of the land here, men whose very blackness syncopates the ground upon which they walk, have attained to a certain dignity, a *gravitas*, that we who inhabit the modern condition have long since dispelled from our repertoire of gestures. We no longer aspire to the honour of being regarded as a *mekigar*, a man of magic or tribal elder . . . indeed a saint! Muslims, I know, regard this special quality in a man as being god-given, a dispensation they call *baraka* (blessing). How is it we no longer wish to breathe in this pure archaic ambiance which for many nomads is the very stuff of life. They will go down on their knees in the presence of a Master. They will whisper incantatory prayers in the expectation of his everlasting life. They will ask for his blessing in the hope that their own lives might be enhanced. Such things I have witnessed while living among those whose instincts are finely attuned to the special beneficence of grace. I know also that true men derive their feeling of fraternity from the knowledge that they all partake of what the great Mevlana called the 'element of congeneity' which draws one man to another.

Therefore, I must inform you, living in a wild state has its own compensations. Here rock, cave, a pool in a river, even a sun-blasted gum tree retain what these nomads call *djang*. It has taken me some time to understand what *djang* is, since the word is always used in the context of something sacred. But, after making a number of journeys in the company of these nomads, I came to realise the expression implied a numinous quality that makes certain landforms more sacred than others. Here the Dreaming ancestors, the Mimi People, and the Rainbow Snake cohabit in a world of myth and symbol. They exist as ochred images on cave walls, in peculiar rock formations, in the echo of water as it tumbles over a waterfall. When you hear the eerie, soundless cry of a Mimi, so stick-like and fragile as it dances across a rock face, then you begin to perceive what it is like to inhabit a truly wild state. The world of the spirit closes about you, caressing you with its closeness now that you have begun to acknowledge its presence.

This, clearly, is what *djang* is all about. My nomad friends have been at pains to inform me such a quality cannot be extracted from the earth as if it was an oyster from a shell. They agree with the great sage who suggested its place is in the placeless, its trace in the traceless. For them *djang* embodies a special power (*kurunba*) that can be felt only by those susceptible to its presence. In this way my nomad friends are able to journey from one place to another without ever feeling that they are leaving their homeland. What they feel in the earth, what they hear in the trees are the primordial whispers emanating from an ancient source. And it is this source, linked as it is to the Dreaming, that they acknowledge each time they feel the presence of *djang* in the earth under their feet.

It may be said of these people that they continually feel the need of what does not exist. We, on the other hand, reject such a yearning as a weakness of mind, a precognitive fear that only serves to undermine the elaborate human edifice we have built for ourselves. But, I say to you, this yearning on the part of my friends is not provoked by fear but by *awe*. They have long ago accepted with joy the role that the possession of a sense of wonder implies. They have no need to ask an object to explain or indeed justify its existence, except in terms of its participation in the cosmic game. Thus water is not made up of hydrogen and oxygen atoms but is instead the great baptismal douche of life itself. The Rainbow Snake proceeds from its watery source and so creates the world. The monsoon rains celebrate a victory over aridity at the end of each dry season and so augment renewal. It becomes evident these nomads are able to lift up the mystery in themselves towards the mystery in the universe. They are able to perceive in themselves something equal to what is beyond them.

I trust this will allay any fears that you may have for my sanity! Nevertheless, for a man to pass over into a wild state he must give up much more than he realises. It is no secret that wildness, by its nature, draws its sustenance from what we regard as primitive. Our incurable domesticity has led us to suspect any movement towards dethroning the intellect in favour of the regality of the intuition. That is why we pay insurance premiums in order to eliminate from our lives the prospect of an accident! Cause and effect become the very stuff of modern existence, governing whatever we do. We are afraid to *risk* anything since to do so implies a failure of the rational intellect to juggle the alternatives.

But in a wild state one is constantly living in danger. On this waterhole I watch an interminable battle for survival being played out each day. Bird, fish, and insect are involved in the weaving of a mighty web of death that is designed to catch all life in its sticky net. Even the giant crocodile, buttressed as it is by what seems like eternity, is able to contribute to this orchestration whenever its jaws are galvanised into action by hunger. Then muscle, bone, and brute strength are drawn into the drama as a buffalo calf bellows out its last breath in the spuming, blood-filled shallows by the river bank. When I see this happen, I know that any causal effect we like to attribute to such an event is far from the mark when it tries to explain the metaphysics of hunger.

As an Oriental sage once remarked, 'Our entire past

exists integrally in our present'. Living in a wild state, however, has made me conscious that the entirety of the past he speaks of is far more extensive than I had previously assumed. It is not a personal past, but one that cloaks us from the very beginning of our collective human existence. He is talking about the profound beauty of sharing our *origins* within ourselves. The primeval ooze is a part of history. We have no need to discredit its role in making us what we are today. Thus dirt is as refined as gold dust, and ashes more evocative of our origins than any well-cut diamond. When we are truly wild we can have no aversion to rubbing dirt on our bodies or decorating our brows with ashes. For these materials are what we are made of at the very moment when we entered into the history of becoming ourselves.

The wild state is clearly a part of a poetic and mysterious universe. Our attempts to understand it on the aesthetic level alone are doomed to failure. My friends tell me that their survival rests not on fragile food resources, but on their ability to enter into the Dreaming whenever they wish. Yet to codify this spirit realm, to chart on a map the contours of the metaphysical land on which they live out their lives, would be to destroy the mystery that for countless millennia they have fought to preserve. Indeed, more than anything, it is this mystery they wish to protect because it signifies to them all the risks they must take in order to retain their primitiveness, their wildness in the natural domain.

So my answer to you is that I now acknowledge how beneficial it is to live in a wild state. Here the borders are made up of seasons, the mating cries of bowerbirds, swallows on the wing at dusk. To cross over into the world of nature is to enter into a condition where one is silently drawn by the stronger pull of what it is one really loves. Unknotting the energy of the sun and allowing it to permeate one's being is to encounter what St John Perse calls the 'high free wave that no one harnesses or compels'. I like the idea of being a part of such freedom, even if it does mean I may have to sacrifice those overly refined sensibilities known only to the eunuch. But we must acknowledge at some point in our lives whether we wish to procreate wonders, or whether we wish merely to adhere to a regime that propagates intellectual insights. I, for one, now know that in conversing with a crocodile, if only in the language of fear, I have begun to intuit dimensions to existence that in the past I would have dismissed. For I realise this animal is not a creature of *anguish* in the way that I have always been. His snouty gaze, rippled as it is by the passage of a dragonfly swooping low over the water, intimates all the untrammelled strength of wildness from which we moderns have shied away.

Does this make sense? Or have I allowed myself to succumb to the lure of allowing my body to become synonymous with the earth? My nomad friends do not think so when they crouch by the fire beside me. They maintain that at last I have divorced myself from the need to observe, to be an onlooker only. In their eyes I am one of them. Under the spell of the Mimi I have entered into the spirit of their land. This, they say, is when a man begins to realise his true heritage as someone who carries paradise within himself. However wild these men might be, however primitive their lives might appear on the surface, I am nevertheless left with a profound debt of gratitude I must somehow repay. At the same time, I am reminded of the words of Marsilio Ficino when he said, 'It is spirit alone I seek, since I seek myself, who am indeed pure spirit'. My friends, in their alliance with those forces of wildness, have made this the basis of their own conduct. I suspect it is up to me now to embark upon a new journey of my own in order to discover the *djang* within myself.

And, finally, I ask you to listen to the pleas of one of your own famed exemplars. The poet, Gerard de Nerval, gave his life in pursuit of the lost paradise within himself. Had he found it he would have realised the verity of his own words when he wrote in 'Vers Dorés':

> *Respecte dans la bête un esprit agissant:*
> *Chaque fleur est une âme à la Nature éclose,*
> *Un mystère d'amour dans le métal repose,*
> *'Tout est sensible!' Et tout sur ton être puissant.*
> *Crains, dans le mur aveugle, un regard qui t'épie:*
> *A la matière même un verbe est attaché . . .*
> *Ne la fait pas servir à quelque usage impie!*[1]

Putting matter to impious use is clearly not a crime that my friends feel they are capable of, for they have only a vague idea of its value as an object of wealth. I only hope we may finally find the courage to desist from committing this crime ourselves.

Your good friend

NOTES

1. Gerard de Nerval. Translation by James G. Cowan.

> *Respect in all animals an active spirit:*
> *In Nature each flower is a soul in bloom;*
> *In metal the mystery of love broods;*
> *'All things feel!' Its power is upon you.*
> *Heed the blind wall its watchful gaze:*
> *Bound to the heart of matter is a voice. . . .*
> *Make matter serve no use that's impious!*

TWO

ON TOTEMS

Dear friend,

Of late I have found myself in a quandary as to my true identity. This is not to say I have become confused in any way; merely that I have begun to ask myself about the *nature* of identity. It is true we suppose ourselves to have an unchangeable personality which we regard as our 'identity'. I have no quarrel with this condition, least of all when I consider that to be identified in such a way makes it relatively easy to move about within the context of this world. No, the identity I speak of is one associated with the existence of *another*—a person or an object which has the capacity to enlarge my understanding not only of myself, but of all I encounter.

Among these nomads I meet with out here in the wilderness there is a belief that we are made up of manifold

identities. At first this struck me as being absurd. Even if
we are arbitrarily named and acknowledge our birth at a
given place in time, I find it hard to conceive such facts
would be of less importance than those these people associate with a totem and a totemic birthplace. Yet my
friends insist this is so: their totemic existence bestows
upon them a fuller identity than the one that I so readily
assume is mine. How is this so, you may ask? Indeed it is
a question that has troubled me for some time.

Clearly, what is at issue is the depths a man is prepared
to descend into the Stygian waters of his own *imaginative*
life. To declare that I am a certain object, whether this
object lives as I do or whether it possesses a more inanimate existence, such as a stone undulating on a riverbed,
or rain falling at the beginning of the monsoon, or fire
flaming from a tree recently struck by lightning, means I
am able to partake of that object's existence in addition to
my own. It means I have embarked upon a more manifold
existence in keeping with a certain alter ego as rich and
mysterious as the one I have allowed to nest in me. This is
what my friends here consider to be the essence of their
totemic being. For they are themselves in the sense that I
know them and they have also acquired the freedom to
inhabit the imagined world of their own particular totem.
Thus when I met an elderly gentleman by the name of
Toby Kangale, I was surprised to discover that he identified completely with the sea eagle. And another friend of
mine, a man called Bill Niedjie, informed me not only was
he a man, but he was also a crocodile!

It took me a long time, I can tell you, to comprehend that
two of my best friends who lived on the edge of these
swamplands were both a bird and a reptile. At first I
merely laughed at their fixation with being something

other than themselves. It struck me such identification was the symptom of a decaying mind, a way of escaping the existential dilemmas of confronting reality as it is. But when I realised they chose to identify with their respective totems because they enjoyed the sense of *enlarged life* it gave to them, then I knew they had no desire to escape the everyday husk of existence I believed was theirs. In fact, it became clear to me, this faculty of identification with their totems excited an imaginative vitality which released in them a new and unbridled energy not available to people such as myself.

How is this so? Well, first I had to discover what my totem might be; what indeed my whole being was drawn to in order that it might lay claim to this larger form of existence. I began, rather tentatively I might add, to explore the environment of these wetlands in an attempt to learn who I might be in the context of something other than myself. You might consider such behaviour no more than a psychological sleight of hand, an act of mirror-gazing for the sake of invoking Narcissus! But, I can assure you, my motives were far more serious than that. My friends here had told me that since I had not received my totem from my father, I must explore to the *limits* of my impressions if I were ever to receive what unfortunately had never been offered me at birth.

So this was the beginning. The world of jabiru, lizard, turtle, and magpie goose became for me the first clefs on an empty page of music. I allowed the timbre of their existence to resonate inside me so that initially what I had regarded as the discordant notes of their wild life, I soon realised embodied a far more composed rhythm than any I might have previously attributed to nature's symphony. The more familiar I became with their habits, the more I was able to wield a baton and thus orchestrate a melody from their movements. It soon dawned on me that all species enact their lives within a field of sound, that they too herald their presence within this open-air auditorium which I had assumed was only here to echo my sense of well-being. The world, after all, is composed of a myriad harmonies, some of which have the power to stimulate what are clearly new arrangements. It was within these new arrangements I began to sense the secret sound waves that would one day enunciate my own totem.

Thus I was able to watch the water-birds swarming in the channel below my tent, listening to their vast cacophony with a new sense of reverence. I say reverence because I had begun to detect in the wading, swimming, diving, and paddling of these numerous species one variegated pattern of activity that seemed, on the surface, to be primordial. How else could I measure the profound effect all these delicate ructions were having upon me, but in recognising in them the *patterns* that now lay in my path? Indeed, this endless swamp of life, this seething cornucopia of blood, bone, and feathers was engaged in some further delineation of existence more explicit than any implied by individual genus. I had come to the conclusion these water-birds were a part of some imaginary body whose visage was formed in the likeness of an angel.

Dear me, you may say! I have clearly taken leave of my senses. Precisely. For the first time I have begun to look at egret, ibis, and heron as birds of a more translucent feather. Their outstretched wings embrace the air on landing with all the lightness of being. I have become conscious that they transcend their predicament with the same ease as a man does when he is possessed by his totem. For birds, like men in the grip of their secret exemplar, are able to exist on both the horizontal and the vertical plane. They are capable of ascending from one order of existence to another, just as we are able to do when we consciously accede to what is instinctive in our natures. Here indeed is the answer I have been looking for. Birds, after all, are both messengers of the gods and linguists as well. If we listen closely, we can hear them conversing in a visionary vocabulary all of their own. Oh, wise owl, sharp-eyed eagle, speeding humming bird, or flamingo who makes the sunset redolent with the pinkness of its image, it is you who exemplify a quality that previously I had considered only in the abstract.

The totemic condition, therefore, allows me to partake of innumerable languages. No longer am I confined by the weight of logic inherent in words. Identifying with a bird or animal, tongue of flame, or a cluster of stars is one way of finding a new form of interior expression. When Gregory of Nyssa asked us to look upon the universe and see it in our own nature, he was suggesting to me the kind of dialogue I should be having with nature itself. Not one of classification, exploitation, or violation, but one that suggested an inborn courtesy which is perhaps more in keeping with the language of heraldry than the muttering of mining companies bent on unearthing from the ground some paltry profit.

You see, dear friend, I had decided to embark upon an interior voyage even as I crossed my legs and gazed upon this shifting palimpsest of birds. The extraordinary thing was that I found I did not need to *move*. Inert, and seemingly entranced, I was able to gaze upon nature, conscious that whatever took my fancy could be *me*. And I flew! Oh, how I soared above this wetland, a pelican whose wings barely moved in the warm, eddying air. In the stork's posture I peered over the crumpled parchment of mud at my feet, trying to translate what appeared to be more ancient than glyphs. In reality they were the small movements made by insects, tadpoles, and tiny fish all squabbling over space in the shallows. But, in this imaginary world, I had begun to tinker with images, impressions, the stuff of brainstorms. What was clearly happening to me was a transformation. Like a moth I had begun to emerge from my own chrysalis, my wings still folded in on themselves, my antennae still damply coiled. Yet, for all that, I had become something other than myself. I had entered into the totemic experience with the ease of a snake slithering over rock towards a patch of sunlight.

Paul Valéry was right when he wrote that if each man were not able to live a number of other lives beside his own, he would not be able to live his own life. My nomad friends regard this as their reason for consciously living through their totem, for their totem gives them access to *other* lives, the opportunity to fulfil their own by inhabiting that realm we know of as the imagination. I cannot emphasise how important the imagination is to these people, since they use it as a surgeon does a scalpel to cut away the ephemera of ordinary existence. They recognise that a man, if he truly wishes to be considered as such, must become 'lord of two worlds'. In other words, he must extend his domain beyond that which is entirely of this earth. He must become a pathfinder, a man endowed with silvered wings at his heels, someone capable of transcending the ordinary by way of what is most distinctive in himself. For these people this distinctiveness is best embodied in a totem. I know this because they always speak of their totem in a hushed tone. After all, their totem partakes of what is most *secret* in themselves. Like mistletoe, it draws energy and is sustained by what is most rooted in a man's heart. Yes, you are right, it is his sense of wonder that encourages him to look beyond himself.

How can a man born out of Leda's egg and destined, it seems to wreak destruction on all he touches, possibly enjoy the privilege of living in harmony with himself? The modern condition has made it impossible for us to link up with our 'better half', our twin. Like Helen, we have long since fled to Troy in the arms of an unruly passion. We long to remain the paramour of our own sensations, rather than enter into a more heavenly alliance. This is because we have lost faith with ourselves, the part of us my friends acknowledge is cared for by a totem. For a totem is an embodiment of that 'heavenly twin', Helen's Polydeuces, the young man who glimmers in the night sky, withdrawn yet not aloof, a manifestation of what is eternal. If Helen had listened to her brother, I am sure she would not have caused so much pain and disruption in the lives of those she loved. This is the role of the totem: to endow a man with circumspection, restraint, the power of discernment. Yes, a totem bears the burden of one's conscience!

Well, you may ask, how does one acquire a totem? After many weeks of wandering about this mysterious land-scape, watching buffaloes wallow and lone dingoes pad softly through the brush, I have come to the conclusion you do not acquire a totem, but that a totem acquires *you*. Wherever I look, whatever species of flora or fauna my eyes happen to engage, I am made constantly aware of their singular gaze. You see, these beings are considering whether they wish to entertain me. Imagine when an olive python stops gorging himself on a rodent in order to fix his intentions upon my person! This is precisely what hap-pens when you set out to find your totem. Nature's inhab-

itants respond in a way that suggests their senses have
been stimulated by much more than instinct. For they absorb my presence in their embrace, green eyed and un-
fearing, knowing, as I do not, that I am clearly one of
them.

You may think that I have fallen for the lure of the primitive in my bid to come to terms with alienation. You suspect that when I stumble upon a bowerbird's nest, I see so
many glittering objects collected by this rag-and-bone bird
that I actually believe I have entered an identifiable haven.
Nature is a grand trickster, a cardsharp who adores to
confuse with her antics. This may be so. Yet I am aware of
no ant that does not know how to prophesy rain with the
use of its senses. An entire magnetic mound will pick up
the signals, much as Mary did the divine message of the
Angel. Then look out! As immaculate as conception might
be, rain certainly has the edge when it comes to dissemi-
nating all the vigour of deity to the parched body of earth.
As a result, more totems are born, more exemplars are
made ready to enter into what is clearly our spiritual
womb.

So, do not ask me to send your totem with this letter. I
am not at liberty to ask of nature the secret she retains
solely for your benefit. A totem, after all, is a *singular* thing.
It cannot be purchased over the counter; nor do they spring
like bolts from production lines! It is true frogs might exist
in their millions—but out there, among the reed beds,
poised among so much that is oozing with dampness,
there lies *one* frog whose mucous limbs are ready to launch
the creature into your being. Is this not a gift? To think that
the tenderness of this creature might one day reside in
your consciousness? Of course, this is only the beginning.
Each of us must learn to fondle what is unfamiliar, the

cicatrice of snails, say, or fishes' air bubbles when they gawp, before we can ever begin to know what is right for us.

I wish I could make you believe in this. You, who reside in your elevated tower, who travel about in conditioned air—you who find it difficult to understand the importance of not identifying with things of your own making. It is, in a sense, a disease: amassing valuables that are insured, storing trinkets in bank vaults, placing oneself in debt in the hope of acquiring happiness. And you laugh when I say my nomad friends have managed to amass for themselves a surplus of wealth not in the least bit associated with ownership or possession. Their wealth lies in *existence*, in the freedom they know when a giant monitor lizard breaks clear of the grass and draws them into the chase. Then they find themselves fully engaged in sharing an experience with this animal. Days filled with antiquity, extinct volcanos, prehistoric skeletons, and geological debris—all these are tossed aside in the exuberance of the moment because my friends know they must travel swiftly if they are ever to catch up with their supper!

Simple, eh? To eat what gives you pleasure. The chase, the swinging club, the limp body of death at your feet, a lost breath that returns in slow gasps: such is the capital nomads store up among their memories. They talk a lot about the animal's spirit, knowing it might be the totem of one of their friends. As they do, reverence creeps into their discussion. They talk about the small death-bird that inhabits the lizard winging its way to its Maker at this very moment. They eye its grey skin, the clawed feet, which a few minutes before were bearing it away from their grasp. These are all part of the monitor's being. They will store such impressions and one day celebrate them as a work of art on a cave wall.

You may ask, where is all this getting us? Talk of totems, the mumbo-jumbo of lizards being transformed into art: are these a real substitute for the smooth mechanisms of modern life? How can a pig-nosed turtle replace a bank statement or indeed a dividend? My answer to this is that the countries of the world are suffering from the doom of ever greater debt repayments and the arid pursuit of larger gross national product. Such abstract notions have become more important and real to us than leaves eddying along a path. Today we are more enamoured by statistics than we are of swallows winging their way south. One wise French poet said it is man who is in question, and his reintegration. Clearly, what he meant was that we have become victims of a desire to deliver ourselves from what nature nurtures in our own hearts. Yes, of course—our totem!

And let me say this: you and I are old friends. We have learnt to accept one another's foibles. I grant you your fears, even though I know they are hedged in by health care and pension contributions. You are afraid of dying and look to an *ordered* release from this life. A small hole in a cemetery, the prospect of going forth as ashes, and then a sense of—release! No more mortgage repayments; and who needs a new car? This life you entered in the fond hope of making a big splash has been reduced to an epitaph. But I ask you to consider what might have happened if you had made contact with your totem. This small being within you, this visible echo of your presence that might sit on a branch, it really does have the power to help you transcend such considerations. Because in your totem you never die, but are reintegrated into something far larger. I know this to be true in that all about me in this wetland I am surrounded by other men's totems. They live on, winged and raucous in the wake of the approaching dry season, trying to come to grips with a slow death which is mine as well. But, in the end, I know they have trust in themselves to re-create what is eternal. These collective forms of life in nature make for a profusion of wealth, even if it cannot be calculated in columns.

So I ask you to think about my offer. Join me in my search for a totem. Look to the apple gum or an echidna or even a toothless catfish to embody your heart. Remember, what we are looking for is an imaginative experience that transforms us. We are not looking for a badge that signifies we are members of some club! Could a sugar glider really justify the cost of our membership? I doubt it. Totems simply *are*. They do not ask of you to embark upon a correspondence course in the hope of learning more about them. Become a cockatoo, shout at the top of your voice that you are so very glad to share with this bird its mysterious habitat. Wetlands, forest, mountains, desert—they all offer you the chance to explore what you really are.

Now I know what you wish to ask of me. What is it that I have discovered out here so suited to my own temperament? You are asking me to reveal what is a secret known only to nature and myself. We are in collusion, for indeed our spirits partake of the same substance. First, there is earth. Then there are the seething waters of these wetlands. And what I inhale draws its purity from green leaves taking in all the exhausted airs of my neighbours. From above, I feel the warm-feathered flush of each dawn as the sun rises. I am surrounded by all the ingredients that have made me and my totem. We correspond, two erstwhile wayfarers whose mutuality enlivens. In the mosaic eyes of a spiny-tailed gecko I see tesserae of my own fragmented existence. And for once they are joined! The sumptuous gaze of a tawny frogmouth makes me realise how rich I am. It is therefore wiser for me to reveal how exuberant I feel, and not its source. For to do so would be to unveil what is, essentially, a mystery.

Dear friend, let me remain silent on this issue. When your time comes, I know your totem will unfold within you with all the aplomb of a frill-necked lizard accosting us from its rock. Welcome this encounter and know that herein begins your pursuit of what is entirely anterior to yourself. For there is so much we don't know when it comes to weighing the wax on ducks' feathers to see whether it might keep us afloat.

Your good friend

THREE

ON CAVES
AND GORGES

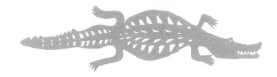

Dear friend,

It is questionable whether you will receive this letter at all since I am writing to you from the entrance to a cave. My friends brought me here in the interest of propriety: indeed, they expected me to *know* where I was even as they left me here alone. For this reason I have chosen to explain to you where I am, in the fond hope, one day soon perhaps, you too will be able to sit at the entrance to what is clearly unfathomable. This cave simulates origins in a way that makes contemplation all but unnecessary. In a sense, I have been left stranded at the entrance to myself, a dumb animal looking for shelter from the harsher elements outside.

This is not to say I am lost. The custodians of this cave are fully aware of my existence. They have simply invited me to partake of a certain solitary condition they deem important when it comes to understanding exactly where I belong. In effect, they have left me in the company of a wide variety of carefully articulated spiritual patterns that take the form of the rock face itself, as well as this cave, dominated as it is by a gallery of ancient paintings, ochred along the entire length of the overhang. So I am not really alone. Solitary, yes, but not alone. By leaving me to my own devices within this purely iconic environment, I suspect that they want me to experience what one celebrated poet called the 'ruined ornament' of my soul. As you can imagine, it is an ornament I have rarely considered worth addressing in the past.

But let me explain. The cave where they have brought me lies deep in an extensive gorge. We had to cross a vast tract of grassland before we happened upon this rather dramatic edifice. Aeons ago this conglomerate of basalt and sandstone must have been thrust up out of the surrounding plain like a cork from a bottle. Imagine the shock of such a cataclysm! Hot rocks steaming in the midday sun, boulders perched among debris like the eggs of monsters! Where once an undulating plain had been, now we witness one of the deepest wounds the earth has ever suffered! When my nomad friends led me along the river bank into this amphitheatre of stone, I knew at once I was about to enter one of nature's most painful scarifications. But I heard no cry of anguish, only the still air filled with birdsong.

On the floor of the gorge a river flows over smooth black stones. In the river snake-necked turtles warm themselves in the sun on small islands. Water bugs dapple the surface with air bubbles. And frogs croak, warning us of the hidden menace of eels. On each side of the gorge the rock face rises sheer to the sky above. In the morning the sun creeps down the sandstone, a gold grimace of light as it pushes back the shadows. Eucalypts cling to the cliff edge above, their mesh of branches far too transparent to conceal any mysteries from us. While on the floor of the gorge itself, palms and poisonous cycads, known as zamias, rise from the undergrowth, their spiny heads a veritable pincushion of leaves.

That is not all. Throughout the valley grow a profusion of shrubs. These compete for my attention with the kangaroo grass, each blossom a splash of colour which makes easy identification impossible. This is because I am overwhelmed by their sheer *variety* rather than by any desire to single out one species in preference to another. I am incapable of recognising species that are clearly *named!* It is obvious that if I were an ornithologist or an orographist or possibly even a palaeontologist, I might find myself better equipped to reduce what I see to the level of *criteria*. But would the shock of encounter be more exciting?

I suspect not. Our obsession with naming things is born from a desire to categorise all that is visible and invisible. In our time it has reached the point where the act of naming has become an obsession. We also long to quantify our perceptions with the aid of numbers. Imagine—those Pythagorean configurations, known as the Decad, the Music of the Spheres, and the Harmony of Number, have become the progenitors of such mundane variations as Specific Density and Market Profile. What for the ancients was a world richly ordered by the Harmony of Number, say, has become for us merely a system of Quantitative Relations. The act of naming a thing is no longer a part of a myth-making process; it has become a method by which we are able to determine its relation to us.

Who among us has made the journey to Egypt? Who today has spent time in Memphis and Thebes learning the secrets of mathematics or astronomy? I suspect many of us have geared our travel plans around Microchip Valley in California where the true science of numbers is being prognosticised. Yet, out here in the wilderness, reality is measured on one hand, using fingers for numbers! Beyond two hands nomads become suspicious of the accumulation of figures. Knowing the Rainbow Snake as they do, they believe it might be averse to the quantification of its existence. A 'scientific' study of the rock pool from which it is said to appear will not yield it to our senses. Yet a mere five fingers placed over the eyes is a sure way to grace us with its *imaginative* presence because, in the depths of our heart, the Rainbow Snake is One, the purest example of Number.

Anyway, I am digressing. Without doubt nature is filled with inestimable phenomena. Nevertheless my friends assure me the origins of all that we name are mythological rather than scientific. To them a chemical equation does not enhance the reality of an object any more than its visible conformation. But its coming into existence as a story purported to emanate from the Dreaming has quite another effect altogether. Indeed, this magical equation has the power to transform ordinary phenomena into a cherished image by allowing its *qualities* to predominate in a way that renders what is seen as superfluous. This cave, for example, is less a construct of stone resulting from some titanic upheaval than a place of repose for certain mythic realities that were depicted on the walls before time was even thought of.

Absurd, you say? After all, time is the *only* reality according to the way we think. We even equate it with money! We cannot conceive of a reality that predates the beginning of time, hence our obsession with quantifying what is transitory. We have forgotten what it is like to encounter the eternal. We gaze at nature as if it were a clock ticking away in some time bomb. We want it to go off because in that way we can be sure it has, at the very least, an economic reality and thus an existential life span. This may be why we are in so much of a rush to dig up sacred ground in our search for minerals, or unleash pesticides on crops. It appears we cannot bear to see nature existing within a timeless vacuum; we would rather see it yield far in excess of its own capacity for renewal than to lie there, a lazy reptile filled with all the hibernatory tendencies which make winter such a special event.

I know what you're thinking. Sitting in this cave has caused me to hallucinate! I see shadows on the walls and confuse them with the torsos of spirits. I regard the ochred hands of men splayed before me as if they were individual signatures. I simply refuse to see things as they are, and am always trying to find means by which an ordinary image might be transformed. Is this such a crime? If a man of talent prefers a rose garden or the sound of a harpsichord to what he is able to imagine, then he is doomed. In the same way, he must never chain his heart to anything he does not love. For to do so is to place himself at the mercy of order, a concept as mangy as any flea-bitten dog, as I will explain.

Order, you say? I dare to speak of order when it's plain to see I have chosen chaos as my helpmate? Well, why not? Even our beloved scientists now speak of chaos lurking below the smooth surface of Newtonian physics. Subject his laws to undue pressure and the Rainbow Snake of chaos erupts from the deep recesses of its rock pool and claims the tribesman who dares to want to look. That is why the hand is so important, for its numerical valency (five fingers, all closed) makes it possible to actually *conceal* from our eyes the full horror of such chaos. Or is it beauty? I am beginning to realise chaos is at the root of all beauty, a fleshy mandragora of branches that nevertheless deceives us with the illusion of being a human body. If a poisonous plant can duplicate the form of our own special grace—why then can't chaos create that illusive beauty we associate with order?

Let's take it further. On the wall of this cave, among all these myriad hands, an image of the Rainbow Snake squirms its way. For my friends the Great Snake is blessed with a contradictory personality. On the one hand it is the maker of all things, a world creator and source of life. Furthermore, it has graced this world with all its quixotic beauties, however diverse we know them to be. On the other hand, this fabulous creature is capable of maleficent acts which even my friends find abhorrent. They are aghast when it eats their own kind and then vomits them up again on the bank. Its penchant for cannibalism fills them with disgust. They often ask themselves why the Rainbow Snake juggles so easily beauty and baseness. Nor do they find a ready answer, either. Except to acknowledge that the Great Snake's character is rooted in chaos, a purely divisible force which, nevertheless, is always yearning to *overcome itself*. In the act of destruction the Rainbow Snake is succoured by what we dislike most. Indeed the Great Snake derives its primordial vitality from the most mysterious principle of all—that of uncertainty.

I know I am treading on thin ice. You will tell me I have lost all capacity to discern the difference between order and chaos. To suggest they are one and the same is to commit a sacrilege. But I ask you: is it not you who commit the greater act of impiety when you suggest that order is paramount? Let me put it another way. If order were a straight line in contrast to something indeterminate and wavy, then listen to what one of our reputable scientists has to say:

> . . . the straight line leads to the downfall of mankind . . . It has become an absolute tyranny . . . something cowardly drawn with a rule, without thought or feeling; it is the line which does not exist in nature. And that line is the rotten line of our doomed civilization. Even if there are places where it is recognized that this line is rapidly leading to perdition, its course continues to be plotted . . . Any design undertaken with the straight line will be stillborn. Today we are witnessing the triumph of rationalist know-how and yet, at the same time, we find ourselves confronted with emptiness. An aesthetic void, desert of uniformity, criminal sterility, loss of creative power. Even creativity is prefabricated. We have become impotent. We are no longer able to create. That is our real illiteracy.[1]

By implication, then, order is sterile, a vicious parody of what we wish to see. It has given us the light bulb, true, but in the process has destroyed what is luminous. My nomad friends are adamant on this point. When we sit around the fire at night they maintain that the stars we see overhead are not mere asteroids fixed in their orbits, but are objects which have the capacity to enliven our intellects. They are not interested in the speed of light which so readily transmits the scintillance we see, but rather the invisible light these stars bestow upon the *conduct* of their lives. This is why they wrap the existence of the Pleiades in an elaborate myth, for they know that in doing so they have superficially ordered what was once a random moment of chaos in the creation of the heavens. What myth does is make comprehensible what is no more than a frozen moment in the infinitely slow deliquescence of existence.

Perhaps that is why I have been left alone in this cave. I have been left in the presence of innumerable generations of men who have attempted to ponder the nature of reality. In turn they have placed their outstretched hands on the wall and blown red ochre around the outlines to register their own amazement. They perhaps understood as little as I do this curious metaphor which passes for life. I mean, of course, the womb! For in this cave were we not all born at some point in time? I am beginning to suspect where I sit is the fulcrum of the world, a huge hearth whose abundant heat is still capable of igniting those pyres we thought had gone out. This is what the Rainbow Snake sees as the fiery nature of myth, the incandescence of its own self-creation. You see how easy it is to allow this cave to do its work! My friends must have known it was the perfect antidote against the venom of intellectual conceit. Yes, it's true. I had long ago allowed myself to become poisoned by the scepticism of this age. Knowing how much I was a victim, I suspect the custodians of this cave wanted me to experience for myself the pure act of rebirth that they have long known it to contain.

Boomerangs exist here as outlines on the wall as well, along with warriors' clubs, emu nets, and delicate vaginal shapes cut in the rock. The latter are stroked with the end of a stick, or a stone knife, whenever a tribesman wishes to invoke the spirit of rain. For he sees in female genitalia the perfect embodiment of fecundity! No other part of the body is so deeply embedded in the idea of abundance. Thus, by stroking this stony appendage, he is able to make a ritual out of orgasm in keeping with the greatest act of fertilisation of which the earth is capable. For him rain masses on the horizon in response to such a demonstration of love. Dampness embraces what is dry all around in an act of coition that dispels aridity in yet another pleasurable moment for us all. In doing so the tribesman is able to ensure the cave wall, bearing its endless hierography of pudendas behind me, remains a sensual monument to all that is fructive on earth.

Is this so difficult to understand? Or does the cave suggest to you darkness? Caves, rock, ochred images on walls, incantational spells—these are no more than disquieting echoes of *where we have come from*. As if the inner dynamics of nature were in some way linked to a point of departure and a destination! Is this not a convenient myth to which we moderns so guilelessly subscribe? Are we not enamoured by the prospect of going *somewhere?* We are in the grip of a monster more formidable than any Rainbow Snake. For the monster that strangles us is devoid of any metaphysical significance whatsoever. It takes on the disguise of 'progress' and simulates excitement by way of gaudy ephemera and what science continually celebrates as 'new' discoveries. The scientists of today triumphantly announce their delineation of the 'edge of chaos' in the computer graphic images of Mandelbrot and Julia sets[2] but this turns out to be little more than a very old chaos which has been symbolically ordered in nomad sandpaintings, arabesques, mandalas, and in pieces of majuscule script from the Book of Kells for a long time. Unfortunately, such 'simplified idealisations of reality', that the scientist speaks of with evident pride, draw their beauty from an abstract mathematical principle rather than anything our spirit might turn to for real sustenance.

I know what you are thinking. If Pythagoras considered numbers sacred, then why am I so suspicious of contemporary mathematics? Did not Rimbaud himself argue that today's idea of progress was bound up with a vision of numbers? Yet when I hear of an eminent professor from a European university declare that he is 'convinced that the rationality of science, expanded properly, is the sole and all-embracing source of cognition for mankind, the only religion of an enlightened future'[3] I know how denuded the scientific mind has become. It is clear some men long to embrace logic as if it were the most alluring siren of all. They succumb to its seductive wiles, masquerading as it does in the garb of the rational intellect, content to believe it alone holds the key to unlocking nature's mysteries. Any mishmash of mysticisms that suggests otherwise is consigned to the ash-can of history, along with so many systems of thought and belief which these men consider to have outgrown their use.

Dear friend, this is my dilemma. My heart warms to the marvellous configurations I see before me in this cave. The gorge into which I have travelled to reach my destination is filled with such a variety of affinities I find it difficult to know where to begin. Should I record their genus, or merely drink in all their mutations to which chaos so readily subscribes? It is a question that troubles me because it goes to the very heart of what I have been trying to say. Either I register *criteria* and so identify with the order that is assumed, or I encounter every exaggeration in what I observe as symptomatic of the hidden chaos upon which nature seems to thrive. On this point my friends are certain, for long ago they have come to the conclusion that the Rainbow Snake, canny Spirit that it is, prefers to remain at the bottom of its pool in a state of formlessness rather than subscribe to the limits imposed by manifestation.

I ask you, then, which path should I take? There is no clear-cut answer. After all, there is a purity about numbers which is heaven-sent. Yet, here in this cave in the heart of a gorge, I am conscious of how easy it is to dispense with number in favour of feeling. In feeling there is a sense of unity; yet I know also that unity is associated with the numeral, One. So where does this leave me? Do I count the leaves on a zamia, knowing it is poisonous? Do I consult the Rainbow Snake whose bountiful coils are capable of hugging me to its bosom? Or do I finally dismiss the polite mechanisms of modern existence (where comfort is contagious!) and reach out, like the hand stencils behind me, for what is, not surprisingly, ungraspable? The real question is whether I have put enough ardour into this enterprise in the first place!

So you see, I am no more resolved now than I was at the beginning. Rather deliberately, I suspect, my friends have left me here to ponder on the true nature of chaos. All I have to guide me is the vast ochrous map on the wall behind. Other men's hands indicate provinces I have not yet had the opportunity to inhabit. Yet I now know these are the frontiers I long to explore in future. For the palm of a man's hand is etched with destiny, experience and character, all qualities which have the power to overcome disorder. Like crumbling papyrus it gives account of certain verities time has nearly erased. These, I'm sure, pertain to the journey a man makes in search of sanctity rather than certitude. Which means what we know as 'chaos in matter' reflects a formlessness that is sacred, a font of blessedness no one should ignore. Let me assure you, my friend, the custodians of this cave have no intention of doing that!

But I must not linger too long here, sitting alone outside this fissure in the wall of the gorge. Like an oracle the cave entrance behind me beckons. Since my friends are not due back for another week, it behooves me to investigate their world more thoroughly—if only as an act of courtesy. For it becomes obvious to me that in wishing to understand the mysteries of nature more deeply, I am able to offer my impulses towards perfection with far greater vigour than in the past. It would be a fine thing if you dropped everything yourself and join me—here in this gorge, among all this basalt and these poisonous cycads? Together we could plumb the depths of the cavern, whereby we might discover new beauties hidden away from the light. In turn we can share them, and thus discover what true brotherhood is all about.

Regards, dear friend

NOTES
1. Friedensreich Hundertwasser, *The Beauty of Fractals,* H. O. Peitgen and P. H. Richter, Springer Verlag, 1986.
2. Ibid.
3. Professor Gert Eilenberger, University of Cologne.

FOUR

ON MYTHS

Dear friend,

Forgive me for not replying to your last letter earlier, but I have only just returned from a visit to the Hole of Life. This probably strikes you as odd or indeed indicative of my recent derangement. When the man you believe you know so well, and the man I might have thought I recognised, acknowledges that he has visited a place known to these tribemen as Bidi, or the Hole of Life, then it is plain he has crossed over the boundary which divides the rational world from what is clearly insensible. No, I am not a shade! But I do now understand that Odyssean predicament whereby a man must confront the ghosts of his former selves if he is ever to become a prophet.

It was on a vast water-hole known as Cullymurra that I first encountered the bones of the Kadimakara, those pri-

mordial creatures who experienced the collapse of their
world many aeons ago. The place happens to be the larg-
est water-hole in this region—so large it is no wonder they
call it the Hole of Life. To reach it, I was forced to cross a
stony desert whose only noticeable features were the petrified skeletons of certain prehistoric mammals and reptiles. Like a junk-yard full of abandoned cars these giant
skeletons reminded me of a time when animals lived a
more fulfilled existence, free from the threat of extinction.
Their very *largesse* assured them of a place in the mind's
eye, where all true myth is carefully fabricated.

By the time I reached Cullymurra water-hole I felt I had
indeed crossed over Homer's blood-filled trench. An air of
unreality filled my waking moments as I trudged along
gullies and over sand dunes. The night sky, too, was littered with the images of beings whose celebrated exploits
on earth had been fixed for all time in stellar orbits. Each
starscape, my friends informed me, recalled an event in
the history of their favourite Sky Heroes. These moments
of creation were reinvented by them each night simply by
gazing up at the luminosity of countless asteroids. No
wonder they were never at a loss for a story when we sat
around our camp-fire at night. For them the night sky was
an undiminished mass of paragraphs, since each star cluster outlined a myth!

In keeping with the respect that we shared for one another, they soon made me privy to their secrets. This was
the first time I can recall they chose to reveal to me how the
world was created. Now you might think this to be no
more than a willingness on their part to shed light on what
for them, as for us, is plainly a mystery. Formulating a
theory of creation is one way of clarifying the confusion we
all harbour towards the mist-veiled nature of our own or-

igins. Whether we espouse the theory of the Big Bang or resort to the jargon of molecular biology, the difficulty of penetrating the mystery always remains the same. Indeed I have come to the conclusion there really is no essential difference between describing the principles pertaining to DNA and giving a mythological account of the cataclysm that confronted the Kadimakara before time even existed. Each partakes of a degree of faith in what, finally, is at the mercy of those limitations imposed on us by language.

You see, we only think we say what we think. The reality, of course, is the opposite. The petrified bones of those prehistoric animals I encountered are a case in point. I readily clothed their bones with an *image* which I believed was the form of ancient diprotodons, or giant wombats, as I imagined them to look when they lived on the earth. The truth was I had made an elaborate guess at what these wombats might look like, much as our scientists do when they give us new models which they believe exactly duplicate processes in life. We all like to take so-called objective data and then clothe it in sensible form. But where we differ from my friends is that we actually believe we have uncovered certain truths which transcend any need to be mythologised. In other words, we believe facts contain more truth than poetry.

It is not difficult to resort to empirical observation when it comes to describing the world we live in, its origins, and the laws that govern it. Like many people, I grew up believing implicitly in Darwin's theories of a mechanistic universe whereby the fittest survived because of their superior genetic development. Such a theory amply confirmed the joy I experienced when climbing into a new model car. Clearly the *old* vehicle had been superseded, condemned to a diminished existence in the wake of this updated

model. Darwin's theories supported my feeling of pleasure as I drove about, surrounded by the smell of new
plastic, all-round stereo sound, and the superior mechan-
ics of a more responsive twin-cam engine. For these were
all part of what is known as 'progress', the relentless process of improving things to a point where comfort, not
transportation, becomes paramount.

The newspapers trumpet each new discovery as if it was
the panacea we have all been looking for. Disease, unhap-
piness, infertility, poverty, even death—these have all but
been eradicated, so we are told. But I note there is never
any mention made of the increasing vacuum in the hearts
of men. The hermits of old spoke of *accidie*, a condition of
incomparable spiritual boredom that afflicts men who endeavour to address only their physical needs. Our age,
surely, has made it an article of faith to patch up the holes
in our physical fabric at the expense of what my friends
regard as their indispensable birthright. After all, their
spiritual life is as important to them as the air-conditioned
splendour to which we subject ourselves in our pursuit of
well-being.

But all this is by way of a diversion! What I really wished
to discuss with you was my encounter with the Kadimakara at Cullymurra water-hole. According to my friends,
the desert we had just crossed to reach this oasis was once
a vast region of fertile plains and forests, traversed by
rivers flowing into lakes. Bearing in mind these men have
no written records confirming their observations, I initially
found it difficult to comprehend their opinion that a paradisiacal environment might have existed here in this remote part of the continent. But they assured me the bones
of the diprotodons I had witnessed *en route* were the surest
proof that conditions *had* changed since that primordial

moment. In other words, what I see now as a desert was once a luxuriant region supporting all kinds of exotic wildlife.

Furthermore, they maintained the present clear sky above had once been filled with dense clouds of dust which perpetrated tropical downpours at regular intervals. Great gum trees reached high into the sky, supporting a complex interlace of green life which shut out all sunlight. From this arboreal vault a group of monsters known as the Kadimakara descended in order to feed on the fruits below. To the tribesmen living on the ground such an invasion spelt the end of the world as they knew it. Once these creatures had tasted of the fruits of earth their appetites became insatiable. In time they had eaten all the shrubs, trampled the earth hard, and finally had resorted to eating the giant trees down which they had come. In an ironic twist of fate they had destroyed their one escape route to the heavens!

As a result, the Kadimakara were forced to remain on earth. They wallowed in the lakes, drinking up the water. They ate everything before them while the tribesmen watched with dismay the rapid depredation of their land. Soon the canopy of trees overhead had been destroyed, revealing one great continuous hole of blue sky. The tribesmen named it Pura Wilpanina, or the Great Hole. Meanwhile, the Kadimakara began to die of starvation now that they had eaten up every shrub and bush. In the heaving marshlands of putrefying earth which had once been rivers and lakes the monsters lay down to die. One by one they expired, their bodies slowly petrifying in the relentless sun which their destruction of the natural environment had released upon the earth. Their bones, the bones of the Kadimakara, littered the dry earth as sombre reminders to the surviving tribesmen of what can happen when the natural environment is treated as an inexhaustible larder. What had once been a luxuriant paradise was now no more. The Kadimakara's insatiable appetite had been the direct cause of their own extinction.

For the tribesmen who had survived, the event had been catastrophic. Encountering the Great Hole for the first time had brought with it a recognition of evil. Droughts, windstorms, bush fires, periods of flood, and the intense loneliness that a desert landscape can evoke forced them to live a marginal existence, burdened not only with the threat of their own extinction as a race, but also with the memory of what had once been the paradisiacal environment of their forebears. They were living among ghosts, memories, clinging to the shards of some ultimate perfection so dimly recalled. The monsters from above had eaten everything of value. All that was left to mark the tragedy of these days were the petrified skeletons of the Kadimakara—none other than those of the diprotodons I had encountered on my way to Cullymurra water-hole.

You see now what I mean? The world of science and myth have merged. For it is true our geologists confirm the existence of a tropical paradise in this region, back in the Permian period, 200 million years ago. Clearly the Kadimakara were the prehistoric mammals and reptiles we now classify and exhibit in museums. They had once roamed the region, massive beasts whose very size implied herculean appetites. Their destruction of the natural world had imposed upon the early inhabitants a trauma which we still retain today: that the world in which we live is finite, capable of denudation and dispersal in the hands of those with less selective requirements.

The truth is the Kadimakara did much more than destroy paradise. Their adamantine presence on earth forced

the tribesmen living here to evolve *rituals* to combat what
they believed to be the unthinking encroachment made by
such creatures. The Kadimakara were unreflective beings.
Their power was the power of gods; and, like gods, they
had no capacity to reflect on their acts since each act was a
rudiment of creation. It was left to the tribesmen to for-
mulate rituals so as to establish some order out of chaos.
To combat the disorder the Kadimakara had unleashed
upon the earth, it was necessary to build a bridge between
the lower world and the one from where they had come.
When the giant gum trees had fallen and the Great Hole
finally revealed, in all its awful grandeur, then the veiled
world of the Spirit had been forced to retreat even further.
Was it any wonder men on earth felt the need to create
rituals in order to re-establish the link?

At Cullymurra water-hole I was forced to consider the
implications of such a breach with the celestial world. Here
I was, sitting on the bank of the Hole of Life, gazing at the
still surface of a mystery. In the early evening swallows
ricocheted off the water, their outspread wings living arcs
of tawny gold and blackness. One sensed they were small
spirits, perhaps of the Kadimakara themselves, announcing they still inhabited the lower world in spite of their
desire to be somewhere else. Pelicans, so sage in their
movements, swam with glacial calmness. And, in the gathering darkness among the trees onshore, I heard the raucous cries of white-feathered corellas, themselves a group
of old men arguing over a drink in a tavern. Here, by the
Hole of Life, I knew I was in the presence of something
that was far older than time itself. Even the dragonflies
dipped their cellophane wings in salute as they sped towards some secret nook for the night.

The power of this place had inspired in me a state of

reverie. My mind and body were overwhelmed with a feeling of repose. Late model vehicles and air-conditioned offices held little meaning for me at this moment. The tiniest leaf falling on the surface of the water-hole intimated the joy of some unheard-of sound. All about me I felt an invisible energy, almost electrical in its intensity, which seemed to draw everything together into a field of force of its own. Dusk is the time nature reserves to assemble all its plumage solely for the benefit of itself. When kangaroos slip down to the water's edge to drink, then you know that you have experienced a truly benign moment. For these gentle creatures are none other than the Kadimakara in disguise, drinking their fill just as their forebears did when they sucked up lakes and rivers. But now one sensed in their movements an element of constraint as if they had learnt to control their unruly appetites. Clearly, then, nature had realised its *limits*.

In the morning I accompanied my friends a short distance from the water-hole to a place which white people rather speciously called a 'playground'. I was told we were about to visit an ancient Kadimakara site where tribesmen for countless generations had performed rites to palliate the forces of chaos. I knew, of course, such places were sacred to the memory of these tribesmen. Here they were able to perform rituals designed to engender a sense of eternity. In other words, they were able to bridge the gap that separated them from what was *most pure in themselves*. Among an elaborate configuration made up of stones, dolmens, and toas, they had fashioned a model of the celestial world, known to them as the Dreaming, where they might encounter the prototype of their divine ancestors. To visit such a place was to enter a field of force more magnetised than any charged by nature. This, I now realised, was because what has been created for ritual purposes by men intensifies the power in a place more completely than what nature is able to achieve on its own. This accounts for the special feeling of awe we feel when we enter a church or visit an ancient sanctuary in Greece. What we experience is the *collusion* between man and nature in order to evoke the true feeling of reverence.

The variable and often complex geometry of the site caught me by surprise. The circles, crosses, angled lines, and statues could have been the remnants of a mathematical equation more in keeping with a law of physics. Imagine, these early tribesmen had already devised a system for expressing the inexpressible. While we glory in our logarithms, these people revere processes by which they are able to compute the true dimensions of the Spirit! It is as if they have been able to transform their memories of the Kadimakara's destructive reign on earth into something more enduring. I, for one, found myself at a loss to explain why the sacred geometry of the site should be so successful at invoking what we understand as *pneuma*, but it became evident to me that I felt a change within *myself* as soon as I had entered the precinct.

My nomad friends imputed this change to the special conditions imbuing the Kadimakara site. I was informed by one of them that since the site had been created by Sky Heroes at the time of the Dreaming and not by men's hands, there would always be a residue of sanctity lingering about the place. This, as I mentioned before, is called *djang*, a term denoting a spiritual power residing in the place. I can tell you this 'presence' readily made itself felt even if one held little sympathy for the fate of the Kadimakara. Their bones had become icons by which my nomad friends were able to restore to themselves some measure of well-being after their long absence from the place. I realised at once my friends enjoyed the small rituals they performed within the precinct because such acts set them *apart* from the mundane world for a few short hours.

It became clear to me also that the story of the Kadimakara's fateful encounter with the lower world signified far more to these tribesmen than their separation from the paradisiacal state. The Great Hole above them may have implied the advent of certain climactic extremes which had destroyed the world of their forebears, but this did not mean life had lost its savour. In fact, my own encounter with the bones of the Kadimakara made me realise how important it is to accept the *loss* of perfection as inherently salutary. For without the knowledge of evil, would we ever possess the capacity for reflection? I do not think so. After all, we acknowledge that the pure will which is said to belong to angels denies them the opportunity to reflect upon themselves. One poet I know suggested as much:

> Angels (it's said) would be often unable to tell
> whether they moved among the living or dead . . .[1]

Whereas we know how to distinguish between what is and what we desire most.

I must say that I wished you were here to share with me these revelations. Camping by the Hole of Life was an interesting experience. To think we had journeyed so far in order to encounter the rich world of myth. I believe this is what strikes me as so unusual about living in the wild. One is constantly confronted by the *intensity* of experience rather than by its superfluity. Each of us makes a journey into an interior world and thereby enters into a new rela-

tionship with oneself. I suspect this is what Odysseus felt
when he told of his experiences to King Alcinous. In the
process of relating his story of the exile's return, the wanderer demonstrated the art of making ordinary events appear significant. Even if the death of the Kadimakara as a
result of their own insatiable appetites may have been the
story of the gradual extinction of diprotodons, I suspect
that their self-exile from the world above holds a meaning
more in keeping with appreciating a particular mode of
living. You see, the Kadimakara's eventual encounter with
hunger typifies our own unwillingness to abstain in the
interests of preserving harmony and order.

My friends understood the story in this way, I am sure.
Otherwise, why would they have felt the need to make
such a long journey to be near their bones? Ancient rites,
custom, and the words of some time-honoured song
merely reiterated the profound awe that they felt when
they walked about the mysterious geometry surrounding
the monsters' burial site. For here they were in contact
with none other than the numen, with what one early
Celtic chronicler called the 'white law that stirred the seas'.
The same chronicler went on to suggest this 'white law'
would one day become 'God and man', surely an indication of the marvellous collusion which exists out here in
the wild between man and nature. My nomad friends are
adamant when they say that without nature living in them
there is little possibility of ever assuming a true initiatory
identity in keeping with that of the Sky Heroes.

Still, I'm probably boring you with all this talk of bones!
The world is full of skeletons as it is. Whether they are
those of diprotodons or Darwinian evolutionary theories,
what is the difference? Their ancestry is shrouded in the
peculiar darkness we associate with having only a *partial*

view. We can therefore be thankful one of our greatest acquisitions since coming into this world is the power to embrace the realm of myth. Without it, where would we be? Gazing up at the Great Hole, knowing there was no escaping the searing heat of disbelief? No wonder poor Oedipus preferred blindness! He, like ourselves, would rather gaze into darkness than face up to life without noesis. For it is true that without the ability to dismiss empirical information we would be condemned to living in a world circumscribed by what we see and feel. In other words, would we not find ourselves at the mercy of our appetites, cut off like the Kadimakara from the ideal world of our birth? Yes I know now myths are the placenta through which all our spiritual sustenance is filtered.

In the meantime, hold no fears for my safety. Here, in the wild, I am undergoing a metamorphosis of sorts. Though my limbs are not yet those of Osiris, I do feel that any dismemberment I feel is partly attributable to a new feeling for sacrifice.

Your friend

NOTES

1. Rainer Maria Rilke, *Duino Elegies*, The First Elegy, W. W. Norton, 1963.

FIVE

ON
WATERFALLS

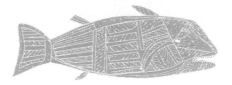

Dear friend,

Yes, I have arrived! The waterfall tumbling over the escarpment before me is like no other: a trembling pillar of white water descending from the sky into the valley with all the aplomb of some lustral fluid bent upon purification. The spray drifts towards me with the slow elegance we associate with a large flag in the wind. Invisible devices are imprinted on the mist, suggesting the blazon on a warrior's shield. For what lies before me is a titular rope leading to the legendary Stone Country beyond—Jack's beanstalk ascending towards the abode of giants who inhabit the realm above. No wonder my nomad friends regard Jim Jim falls with a certain awe. They consider the place to be *maraiin*, or sacred, since it embodies a spirit of its own.

But, let me explain. I was brought here by Toby Kangale, one of my Mirarr friends. Though the region in which Jim Jim falls lies is not his 'country' as such, he possesses visiting rights because of his friendship with the neighbouring tribal owners. Making the journey to Jim Jim was considered to be a necessary excursion in the old days before the white man had chosen to disrupt age-old nomadic patterns. Thus Toby and his friends considered the place to be an important ceremonial site when they were making their Dream Journey each year. It was therefore a great privilege for me to be brought here, knowing that Jim Jim was a place of repose for certain ancestral spirits.

We made the trip in an old Land Rover belonging to Toby. Along a winding, deeply rutted track we drove, through brown savannah country dotted with vibrant sand palms. Sparse scrub broke up the grasslands, and the pieces of black stone filled with iron ore we saw lying on the track gave the countryside the illusion of extreme weight. As we drew near to the escarpment itself, black cockatoos rose from the grass, tiny red feathers in their tails streaking the shade cast by the rock face with a thin trail of blood. When the birds finally landed in a tree to observe us, their black combs so keenly cocked forward reminded me of the headdress worn by Hawaiian chieftains dressed in ceremonial garb.

As we drove inland I became conscious of entering an ancient world. Even dead tree stumps, some burnt out by bush fires, revealed a richly patinaed wood whose grain and knots merely contributed to the intricate designs confronting us. In the distance, a scrub fire moved on a wide front, sending up a thin line of smoke and flames which threatened to cut us off from our objective. Luckily, Toby knew the route well and was able to make a detour around the conflagration. This did not stop kangaroos, wallabies, emus, and giant monitor lizards scurrying to safety among the rocks and enclaves along the escarpment.

I suppose the threat posed by the bush fire heightened our own sense of being cut off. There was nowhere for us to go but forward in the hope of reaching our destination safely. The trouble was, I did not know where we were going! I had placed myself in Toby's hands on the basis that Jim Jim falls was worthy of my visit. To risk life and limb in the wild, however, is very much a part of reaching an unknown destination, especially when the destination promises to be as secretive as any lost oasis in the desert. Toby's description of the place was so evocative that I was keen to risk *all* in order to gaze upon a place his people considered sacred.

So, you see, I have taken it upon myself once more to confront a condition that for many of us does not exist. I mean, how does one explain the need to enter the folds of nature in pursuit of some ineffable state known as *maraiin?* I realise this excursion of mine smacks of the absurd. Why should a remote waterfall, whose only claim to fame lies in its capacity to *overflow*, be in any way significant? I don't know. Nevertheless, I am prepared to place myself here, at the matrix of this immeasurable moment, simply to gaze upon such a brimming verticality of water. In the act of falling from the river above, the water has broken with its state of fluidity in order to absorb, for a short time, those infinite variegations of light sunlight enjoins.

Jim Jim falls is the only source of water that deigns to descend from the escarpment above. Those who live at its source are known by Toby and his friends as the Stone People. This is because they prefer to live among the boulders and rock outcrops on the plateau above rather than descend to the grassland below. The only link between these tribes is the waterfall upon which both peoples rely for their survival. It is not surprising, therefore, to discover that each tribe regards Jim Jim as important to its well-being. To the Stone People it acts as a conduit, releasing to a wider world beyond the full beneficence of its excess. While to the tribesmen below, Jim Jim provides them with a link between the beautiful and the necessary. What they witness is an object whose miraculous conformity perfectly engenders the function it fulfils: that of falling!

Let me describe where I am. Above, the escarpment rises sheer in multiple layers of heat-folded rock. Small shrubs grow in the rock face, stubbling the stonework so that it looks as if it has not shaved. In the vicinity of the waterfall the rock is stained black by millennial dampness. Around the pool below wattle trees grow, their yellow blossoms as vibrant as the wings on butterflies. These, too, hover above the pool and gasp at the beauty of their own reflections, just as water-smooth boulders grapple with their dimensions on a sky-laden surface. While the sound of falling water begins to echo at the very heart of all this stillness, as an unhurried patter, restrained, yet filled with intimations of timelessness. Like a pendulum it swings from side to side, measuring space with the lassitude of an elephant observing the swaying of its own trunk..

But that's not all. Tiny gargoyles of stone protrude from the rock face upon which birds perch and contemplate what is their idea of solitude. Occasionally they cry out, perhaps overwhelmed by their feeling of exuberance in the face of so much that appears ordered. When a feather spirals earthward it is a signal that one of these birds has acted in accordance with its nature, expelling a quill with which its own flight is assured. No wonder we are drawn to such objects when we find them on the ground. Their form and seeming fragility remind us flight is something that even we aspire to, in spite of our own unwieldy natures. What birds do with such ease, soaring through space, supported only by the interaction of their wings with the air, we can emulate only in our imagination. Show me the man whose mind has not flown over the abyss and I will show you someone who has forfeited his right to dream. For when we are loaded with life and almost embarrassed with our surfeit of freedom, we often forgo the pleasure of rising above our difficulties for fear of tumbling to our deaths like the legendary Icarus. Nevertheless, we can learn from the birds when we ascend into nothingness: be aware that what is invisible is often more supportive than the things we know and understand.

That's all very well, I hear you saying. It might be pleasant for me to engage in a colloquy with nature, devising a language out of the muteness of being, but where does that get you when it comes to dealing with everyday existence? How can a man learn the language of the birds when he already has trouble comprehending those abstract forces which continually threaten his own being? And speaking of these, why are birds exempt from the harsher aspects of economic servitude? Why is it they do not pay taxes, keep bank accounts, or imprison themselves in those cages of credit to which we are prone to sentencing ourselves? Is it because they live wisely, in accord with their true nature, or is it because we have allowed ourselves to become victims?

This journey to Jim Jim falls is an acknowledgement of my own confusion, but I am prepared to travel to the very *limit* of this world if it means I may discover for myself why we have so easily succumbed to this mania for certitude. What has happened to the mysteries? Why do we wish to measure everything in terms of money or statistics? Graphs of figures and market projections are a modern variant of the animal entrails poured over by the soothsayers of old. It's simply that we prefer to read graphs as we have faith in their ability to yield truths of a quantifiable kind. No wonder we become downcast when they tell us we are on the 'downturn', or that we can expect our circumstances to become 'depressed'. These predictions are the result of computations devised by present-day wizards who seem to be bent upon perpetuating their skulduggery on us all merely for their own profit.

My answer to you is to ignore the antics of these pseudo-occultists! They prey upon our fears, knowing full well we are thoroughly averse to confronting our own insecurities alone. They speak of interest-rate hikes, debt repayment, and overseas deficits in the way others in the past might have spoken of plagues and pestilence. The trouble is, we find ourselves afflicted with a disease brought on by *abstract* notions rather than any we can identify by their organic symptoms. Clearly, it is a failure of the imagination on our part which causes us to feel so ill at ease in the wake of doomsayers promulgating their particular brand of disorder. In contrast, I offer you this thought: solitary harmony offers to the self-intoxicated soul a more delicious liberty than any that might come as a result of sound financial investment.

My nomad friends are conscious of the investment they must make in the interests of their own well-being, though they measure this not with figures, but with a sound inner knowledge borne of a respect for the past, and for tradition. In principle, they have little interest in the new, except where it is eminently practical. Thus they look upon a place like Jim Jim falls as being a spiritual warehouse where age-old intuitions are permanently stored. They come here to stock up on those invisible perceptions the waterfall constantly echoes. In the presence of tiny, black-striped fish and larger cobalt-coloured ones, they too are able to drift under submerged stones, feeling the glory of weightlessness as it pertains to their own soul. For, there is no doubt, the unique and eternal movement of the soul is towards that which does not exist. What was and is no longer, what will be and is not yet—these are its real concerns: never that which *is!* Always remember, chance is on your side in this engagement. It changes insensibly into wisdom as you pursue it through the labyrinth of your being.

But, enough of this! I came here with Toby Kangale in the hope of being exhilarated. Truly, a pillar of water is a divine thing, embodying small essences of spray more in keeping with the fervour of grace than with the act of *descent*. And when falling water emits a rainbow, then you know it has entered into a state of efflorescence. Saints' bones are reputed to emit the sweet smell of myrrh on occasions such as this. What is the difference? Each is engaging in a miracle of transmutation whereby their interior natures have cause to celebrate their very existence! But, you say, they are dead. Saints' bones and rain water are about as animate as tombstones. I tell you, if ordinary spray can transform the actual invisibility of light into all the colours of the spectrum, this surely is clear evidence of a lively occurrence!

I have chosen to lure you through all this maze of wildness in the hope you too will discover a thread. No, I am not the minotaur, that bullish being craving to consume seven pure young men and women in order to satisfy my inordinate hunger. But I do sense we have chosen to contain all this wildness within ourselves under the pretence that somehow it can be neutralised. For what does the idea of remaining 'civilised' mean in the context of living in our huge cities of today other than this? I suspect it really means we have chosen to revert to an isolated state simply because we have lost the sense of fellowship in the conduct of everyday life. When we relied on *other* people, then we were always alert to their urgent needs as they, in turn, relied on us. Remaining civilised is determined by the continued existence of a level of wildness within ourselves. Without it we are condemned to living at the centre of a confusing labyrinth of desires, at the mercy of our own hunger to consume rather than to enjoy what is pure in the world nature offers.

All this is by way of telling you how easy it is to succumb to the tingling sensation caused by a fine mantle of spray settling upon my face and limbs. Toby says this is the cooling breath of the Rainbow Snake as it bathes us with its invisible presence. I know I have become aware of the terrible proximity of the Divine Serpent's *absence* in the pool below the waterfall. You can almost hear the beast pearling the surface of the water with the perturbation of its submarine existence. Bubbles! How they dance before my eyes, small scintillations of light in keeping with the vaporous appearance of the Sky Hero whenever it decides to move among us. No wonder Toby speaks to me in barely a whisper. What he witnesses with the eye of his heart causes him to feel reverential to the point of *fear*. Ah, awe: it creeps up on us from behind, cozening us in its coils, squeezing from us all that is trivial. Clearly, awe is the pressure we subject ourselves to in the hope that the soot in our souls will one day glimmer like diamonds.

Dear friend, I am not asking you to believe all that I tell you. But life in a rock pool is no laughing matter! When you see the dark curving tail of a fish drift in and out of your vision it's as though you are witnessing something in the act of falling asleep. Coruscations of moss on rocks underwater cling to the bubbles made by tadpoles. There is drowsiness here: only the water spiders are adamant their trackless paths upon the surface lead to a more secluded haven. No web contains them since they have long ago extended their terrain beyond the one to which we cling. Imagine, the art of walking on water we attribute to gods and certain saints, yet this insect applies itself to the journey with all the aplomb of an avatar walking towards us! Do we have that kind of faith? Or are we buoyed up by the illusion that such acts of levitation are part of a spurious condition fit only for those who desire to escape?

Here, in this massive concavity of stone, I hear all the echoes from the world above. The Stone People have left their mark. What descends from above is but slender evidence of the mystery surrounding their lives. Do they bathe in the river, watch for pig-nosed turtles as they plop off islands to escape their clutches! Who knows. Toby says they live as his people do, but I suspect he is concealing something from me. Secretly, I believe, the Stone People abut one another, as secret signatures of life, in keeping with the sheer *hardness* of their own culture. Their dances belong to them alone; so too do their songs. Thus they are able to intensify the level of reality that surrounds them by way of dream-songs like this:

> *Forked stick and rafters, floor posts*
> *with a roof like a sea eagle's nest*
> *lie by a billabong where goose eggs*
> *give the water its huge expanse.*

My people build, thinking of rain—
rain and wind from the west, clouds
slowly spreading over the billabong—
while we raise our grass huts.

Our chests heave like clouds
as we call out for the rain to fall.
Rain! dampen us with your deluge
as soon as we build our shelters.

I know this sounds like a poor excuse to embark upon a real estate investment, but to the Stone People the prospect of the wet season catching them unsheltered is a real threat. They long for rain so that their land may be renewed, yet equally they know it will condemn them to extended periods of lethargy as they lie about waiting for the rain to stop. The sound of thunder, hours of torrential rain, a dark sky vividly blanched by lightning—these they will witness as they sit together in their huts. The puddles in the clearing will be a mass of dimples as the rain continues to fall. Swollen rivers will break their banks, the waterfall before me will begin to cascade in an ever-widening concourse. The animals of the bush—the sugar gliders, possums, echidnas, bandicoots, and wallabies, to name a few—will find shelter under rock ledges and in caves or deep in the heart of trees. For the wet season (*Gudjewg*) signals the beginning of a time of renewal that affects not only the land, but also life in the estuaries of the rivers and along the coast. Even crocodiles are conscious the water tastes fresher after the stagnant draughts they have been used to during the dry season.

So now, I hope, you begin to understand how important Jim Jim falls is to the people living in this region. It's not just an overflow point that relieves the escarpment of its abundance. Toby insists it is the source of the ambrosial juice upon which the Rainbow Snake thrives. Orchestrated by Yagjagbula and Jabiringi, those venerable Lightning Brothers through them the whole earth receives its baptismal bath. Their Promethean struggle is the epitome of all great natural encounters. For only when a storm breaks does one sense that there is discord in the heavens. The world watches, the world listens. Above us, a veritable ocean of water is suspended. It is only when the two brothers begin to fight that the celestial dam is threatened. And then the first raindrops fall, sweat of the Sky Heroes, the residue of their titanic struggle against the powers of aridity and drought. While we who sit below, nomads and visitors alike, smell the air as it intimates a downpour. Even the bush exudes a perfume in the wake of the humidity that first touches our brows.

I know what I say makes you smile sometimes. But when next you start your air-conditioned car and drive home through the pouring rain, think less of the inconvenience it causes you and more of the invisible forces that make it possible. For you, too, are as near to the Lightning Brothers as I am. The rock pool haven of the Rainbow Snake below Jim Jim falls where I am now is as near to you as the washbowl in your bathroom. Give yourself wholly in your mind to what you see there because it will create in you heaven's greatest gift to us all—that feeling of euphoria, and the ability to make the most of it when it bestows upon you its special grace. Clearly, this is why Toby has brought me here. The long journey through fields of fire, the clouds of smoke that obscured our vision of the track—in the end these were of little consequence once we had reached our destination. Because for many of his people the waterfall embodies what the Sufis of Islam call *dhikr* or 'recollection'. By gazing at such a slender sapience of water, this pure spangle of small collisions, one is able to enter into a state of mindfulness capable of restoring one's sense of well-being.

Surely, my dear friend, this is the realisation of a state for which we all strive. Indeed the true sages, whoever they may be, derive their wisdom and knowledge from nature, just as Jim Jim falls does its aqueous condition when the rain comes. No wonder Toby smiles at me before cupping his hands to drink. His thirst is equal to all those, including myself, who yearn to drink their fill.

Your friend

SIX

ON THE
RAINBOW SNAKE

Dear friend,

My nomad friends harbour a deep nostalgia for the Rainbow Snake. Their every act intimates a preoccupation with the nearness of its immortal coils. Strange as it may seem, the beds of most rivers trace its path across the land at that eternal moment when the world was new. They call this time the *alcheringa* when all forms were in flux and struggling for expression. What a strange feeling it is to reach a slow-moving watercourse and know you are encountering the cicatrice of a spirit! The great outflow from the headwaters are like tears, surrendering their sentiments to a fathomless ocean. According to my friends, the Rainbow Snake has made this all possible in the act of journeying from its *source*.

I first encountered the Rainbow Snake on the walls of a

rock gallery in a desert region known as Mootwingee. Its giant body, painted in red ochre and as rhythmically detailed as a sound wave, reached the full length of a cave, straddling numerous hand prints put there by earlier inhabitants. These prints were like prayers, celebrating the presence of a god. I could almost hear the voices of these people, summoning the snake with their chorus. They seemed to be pleading with its form to release some secret beneficence upon the parched earth of their spirits. Then I realised what they were crying out for was rain.

> Lightning's tongue flashes above cloud
> makes them shine like ochre, bright
> among the shifting yellow cloud.
>
> Rainbow Snake raises its tail
> and from a hole its head appears,
> a flash of light among clouds.
>
> The Snake quits camp, to strike
> strike! the burgeoning cloud,
> lace it with thin streaks of light.

So this was the world I had chosen to enter. My arrival had been auspicious, since the night before I had camped in a dry gully whose sandy bottom had been eerily silvered by the moon. It had been a clear night, and still—so still that a boobook owl widened the silence with its solitary call. The gum trees along the watercourse stood inert, shy sentinels whose leaves reminded me of a thousand swallows' wings. Though I had made the journey alone, I somehow felt in the darkness that the eyes of the bush were absorbing me as they might an interloper. They were watching me, wondering whether my rediscovered sense of wildness was real or induced. I had no answer for them but to gaze into the flames of my camp fire and plead for their patience.

Imagine how I felt when suddenly I heard thunder. In the distance lightning bathed the hills in a grey light. The trunks on the gum trees shone. And then, moving along the gully, I could hear the wind rushing to meet me, a serpentine gust that told me the Rainbow Snake was drawing nearer. I retreated to my tent as the first drops of rain fell. For a long while I lay awake listening to the rain pelting down on the canvas, thinking of the dry earth outside, its empty fissures already beginning to sing in haphazard chorus. I asked myself: is this the beginning of the Deluge? Have I turned myself into one of Noah's sons who gazed upon his father's nakedness with reluctance? Surely I have courage enough to embrace this downpour as I would my father, thankful that his conception of *me* was itself an act of trust.

This might sound strange to you, secure as you are in the habit of viewing water as a mixture of two gases. But I ask you: is it possible to emerge from the instant, compose your powers, and disengage who you are from the living mud which takes the form of a man cast down and abandoned? Indeed there is nothing more morbid, nothing more inimical in nature than to see things as they *are* at a given moment. Such a cold and perfect clarity is a poison impossible to combat except by placing oneself at risk. Among all the intoxications available to us, the noblest, surely, the most resistant to that great tedium we know as certitude, is the intoxication we derive from acts that have a timeless significance. I suspect this was on my mind as I lay in my tent, conscious that after many years the drought had finally broken.

Thus, I was unsure of what to expect in the morning. The damp earth underfoot was as soft as Adam's clay. The leaves on the gum trees glistened. The gully below my tent was awash with water, half submerged branches, and gum nuts drifting off to germinate in soil of a more sappy nature. Galahs screeched, their pink underwings more vibrant than the vigour of their encounter with the morning. Rising above the trees, they wheeled aimlessly, overcome by the clarity of the air. When I finally managed to light a fire to heat a billy, the smoke snaked skyward, a slender tendril of whiteness that slowly dissipated. It was then I realised how ephemeral are the things we see. Nature offers us visions, but we are expected to imbue them with meaning before they disappear.

The journey that morning to Mootwingee persuaded me I had been visited by the Rainbow Snake the previous evening. The world had changed! Clear sunlight garlanded the pathway, causing mica to glitter in stones. I stumbled upon a magpie ruffling its feathers in a pool. Lizards had come out to drink, their horny skin as rugged as shoals in a creek bed. And when I encountered two wedgetail eagles bathing, I was overcome by the size of these raptors. They stood there, feathered monuments each one of them, gazing at me in the same way they might at a rabbit or rodent. In that moment I had become their prey. For what we eat feeds our own good and ills. Each morsel we swallow melts away and soon dissipates within us, bringing new life to our virtues—and, equally, to our vices! These eagles must have regarded me as an attribute of their keen sight, or perhaps their power to glide effortlessly on warm airs.

To be a witness to nature's exuberance can often be offputting. We who are at the mercy of our appetites nevertheless long to render ourselves immune from the demands our bodies make. Was it not Plato who said 'the body, for the sake of which we desire wealth, is the ultimate cause of all wars'? Between this statement and the need to fill our stomachs there lies a vast territory still to explore. Survival, of course, is an exemplary condition. My nomad friends are keen students of existence, often harbouring a storehouse of knowledge pertaining to the business of prolonging it. When Bill Neidjie remarked, 'My culture is hard, but got to be to keep him. If you waste him anything now, next year . . . you can't get as much because you already waste. When I was young I never wasted, otherwise straight way I get into trouble. Even bone not wasted. Make soup or burn that bone. Watch out! That might be Dreaming one too . . .'[1], we find ourselves confronting a level of conservation unheard of among the wilderness of our supermarket shelves. How many trees do we consume manufacturing boxes which we immediately throw away? How much crude oil is converted into plastic that we might discard the bag in which our potatoes are packaged? As consumers our bodies are victims of a wealth we constantly abuse. Abandoning what we produce as soon as it has fulfilled its purpose is the hallmark of a culture which is disposing of itself! No wonder Bill Neidjie despairs when he watches the trucks hauling away yellowcake from the uranium mine on his land. He knows what was once *incorruptible*, the very embodiment of something timeless for his people, is now condemned to a life of exploitation and waste. The land which nurtured his forefathers since *alcheringa* has been reduced to 'raw material' so energy may be generated.

Here lies the rub. Energy is ephemeral and disappears like smoke. It cannot be husbanded for long periods, except where it relies on a natural process to renew itself. Hydroelectricity and wind-driven generators, along with solar heating, are probably the only true renewable energy sources, since they rely on the illimitable power of nature. Digging up 'raw material' from Bill Neidjie's land to power nuclear reactors not only unleashes a dangerous form of energy upon the world, but leaves my friend in possession of a lifeless homeland. Its incipient power, its *djang*, which has continued to mature in the earth over countless millennia, has been hauled away to power factories that manufacture boxes for you and me to throw away at our leisure. What waste! The special sanctity Bill and his forebears have immemorially enjoyed has been converted into a disposable product. In truth, what has been hauled away to fuel factories is the sacred history of a people. 'Our history is in the land; it is written in those sacred places. So you can know and understand'. So says Bill Neidjie, knowing in his heart that his past is being consumed by our inordinate hunger for things, our lack of respect for what is permanent.

So you see, my friend, why the Rainbow Snake is so important to the land. This beast whose home is in the *alcheringa* bears within its stomach stone eggs which, when laid, are the topographic features that my nomad friends identify as 'their' country. The Rainbow Snake has the power to give birth to a physical reality which, in turn, embodies the spiritual landscape of a man or woman. This land *is* the man or woman, whether they recognise it or not. It also forms an aspect of their soul, capable of empowering them with a metaphysical dimension that ultimately derives its origin from the Spirit itself.

To a certain extent, this is what I felt in the air as I came upon Mootwingee that evening. After a day tramping across a pristine landscape made new by recent rains, I could not help being moved by the high cones of rock that confronted me in the dusk light. Entering the gorge, I

experienced the sensation we associate with being on a
train when an adjacent carriage pulls out. The clouds overhead were stationary while the gorge in which I stood was
moving perceptibly! No wonder I felt a trifle giddy when I
reached out for support. For the world I had entered had
overturned my sense of space. Clearly, the Rainbow
Snake, and its host of acolytes on the cave walls, knew
how to *reverse* the process of perception in the interest of
understanding. My giddiness was as a result of feeling the
presence of the *alcheringa* within myself.

You will laugh, I know, at this observation. You will
think me mad for allowing myself to become a victim of
such moods. How can a man whose modernity is acknowledged succumb to such heathen gibberish? But I ask you:
what is wrong with listening to those inner voices which
clamour to be heard above the raucousness of the so-called
real? Surely we are more general than the sum of our life
and our acts, since we are designed for more eventualities
than we can possibly experience. In a sense, our possibility
never leaves us. Our only hope, therefore, is to discover
the means of action which diminishes the bad and in-
creases the good in ourselves. This, in turn, furnishes our
sensibility with the means of acting upon itself, each according to our own nature. Then, I'm sure, we will be able
to rediscover the vertebrate and biped that we are in our
mind! If not, I fear that we will forever remain superficial in
our dealings with the world.

In the morning I began my visit to the rock holes of
Mootwingee. This unusual landform rose out of the surrounding plains, a series of smooth cones formed by tectonic forces deep within the earth. Once a part of an
extensive floodplain, the river has since retreated far to the
east, leaving Mootwingee standing alone, a hard conglom-

erate of stone brittled by frost. As I walked into the first
gully, I sensed about me the giant armorial skeletons of
prehistoric creatures, the Kadimakara of old. Trees and
small shrubs grew in the crevasses, bizarre mutations,
remnants themselves of some ancient order of flora. Red
river gums provided a spindly shade, their trunks scarred
with contortions. Purely anarchic, these trees made no secret of their desire to transcend order and pursue a plan of
unpatterned growth. They too saw themselves as a rough
draft of some tree as yet unborn, just as we dream of being
someone else.

Here I was, then, in the midst of *loneliness*. And, in
this state, I was able to perceive what previously I might
not have considered appropriate: that we do not need
the whole of nature to survive, only part of it. The part
we require, however, imposes a responsibility on us to
communicate with nature, cleansing the atmosphere of
any poisons that might have accrued because of mutual
neglect. Bill Neidjie is adamant on one point: that nature
is watching and listening to us even when we have lost
our sense of awareness. 'Tree, he watching you. You
look at tree, he listen to you. He got no finger, he can't
speak. But that leaf . . . he pumping, growing, growing
in the night. While you sleeping you dream something.
Tree and grass same thing. They grow with your body,
with your feeling'.[2]

The old man, I recall, was certainly clear on this point.
He even went so far as to suggest that when a tree is ailing,
then it is within our power to experience its pain. 'You
get weak . . . little bit, little bit. Because tree going bit by
bit . . . dying'. Oh! To think our limbs conjoin with those
of a tree. Might not the reverse be true? When we are
feeling ill, might not a tree double up in pain? If this were

so, I now know why the red gums around Mootwingee are so individual in their formations. They have experienced the private anguish of so many men who, in passing, have looked for solace among their mute and silvered limbs.

Do you understand what I am trying to convey? Or do my maunderings, burdened as they are by intuitions, leave you incredulous? Ah, the risk! Allowing our minds to deal with the abstract rather than retreating into the smooth shell of what is obvious. No wonder we enjoy identifying with the life of a turtle; this creature can always withdraw into its own familiar world. The truth is, we must learn to break free from what is foisted upon us by outmoded dualisms: the objective warring against the subjective; the economic imperialism of profit and loss; lives shackled to dehumanising tasks that masquerade as 'productive development.' It is these that form the distorted pattern on the shell of our own existence! In contrast, we need to evoke a more rigorous state of mind, as though a life-and-death matter, that is inspired by something insignificant as far as life is concerned.

Yes, poetry.

Poetry, you say? In an age of images of material prosperity you wish to speak to me of poetry? At a time when credit cards are talismans capable of granting us our most frivolous desires, you ask me to embark upon a journey with your nomad friends in the hope of discovering some abstract excitement? I can hear you fulminating even as I write! In any event, words are the source of all misunderstandings, so why should I allow myself to be seduced by a line of verse? My friend, it is not verse I speak of. The poetry I allude to allows us to be insensibly transformed, ready to live, breathe, and think in accordance with a rule and under laws which are no longer of a practical order.

When this happens we have entered the poetic universe inhabited by the Rainbow Snake. Together we are able to stand in a cave here at Mootwingee and marvel at a surreptitious image whose form is god-given.

Take heart. Your world of glass, so reflective and outward, is no different from the water in one of these rock holes. I see myself gazing at the ripples I make with my fingers. These are thrown back in my face in the same way that your bright tie spangles the street where you stand. Self-satisfaction is an easy pool to drown in, whether one is out here in the bush or where you are, cornered on some pavement under street lights. My mind fumbles with the same disordered thoughts as yours, craving verities as immutable as bullion. Hear me out. I am asking you to recognise that the world of the Rainbow Snake is as intrinsic to our spiritual well-being as the down payment on a house.

The problem is we cannot bank it. The Rainbow Snake defies all our attempts to render it practical or make it into a commodity. However much we measure its length, analyse its age by carbon dating, assess it from a stylistic viewpoint, or hypothesise on who might have painted it in the first place, the Rainbow Snake still eludes us. Squirming through the undergrowth of our minds, this reptile evokes ancestral memories which bind us to some distant past, the *alcheringa*. Like an arrow shot into the past with a cord attached, we are able to draw ourselves backward to the image in which it has come to rest, but only when we observe the Rainbow Snake. None of us know quite what it is meant to represent, either. Enigmatic, silent, its length as paradoxical as its shape, this mythical beast somehow squeezes us in its embrace. We are held, our limbs as disjointed as red gums, tremulous, hovering in the space between two opposing worlds. We know the Rainbow

Snake will not speak to us directly, for it is like Bill Neidjie's tree—fingerless. All we can somehow grasp is that we
have entered into what Noah knew as a 'covenant with the
rainbow'. When Yahweh said:

> This is the token of the covenant which I make between me
> and you and every living creature that is with you, in per-
> petuity.
>   I do set my bow in the cloud and it shall be for a token of
> a covenant between me and the earth.
>   And it shall come to pass, when I bring a cloud over the
> earth, that the bow shall be seen in the cloud:
>   And I will remember my covenant, which is between me
> and you and every living creature of all flesh; and the wa-
> ters will no more become a flood to destroy all flesh. And
> the bow shall be in the cloud; and I will look upon it, that
> I may remember the everlasting covenant between Yahweh
> and every living creature of all flesh that is upon the earth.
>   And Yahweh said unto Noah: this is the token of the
> covenant, which I have established between me and all
> flesh that is upon the earth.[3]

No wonder my friends regard the caves at Mootwingee as
important power centres. It is here that the Rainbow Snake
is home to a covenant between man and the *alcheringa*.
Functioning as a bridge between heaven and earth, it allows men the opportunity to address those concerns they
have with the imagined world. Bill Neidjie knows he is in
the presence of a sacred figure, equipped as it is to unravel
his spiritual dilemmas. Rain, of course, is only part of the
problem. Knowing how to conserve the fragile edifice of
his environment makes it imperative that Bill and his people acknowledge the despair waste can provoke in a man's
heart. Husbanding the land's resources is as important to
them as looking after their own well-being. This knowl-

edge is inborn, the harvest of many aeons working together. Nature may be mute but that does not mean it has nothing to say. Translating its signatures becomes the task of all men in collusion with the Rainbow Snake itself.

Dear friend, forgive me for troubling you like this. Much of what I have to say you may regard with the same distaste that you might a computer virus! But I ask you to consider this: intensity of being is reserved for all those who are prepared to embrace the wild state within themselves. Acknowledging the Rainbow Snake is a part of breaking down the barriers that exist between ourselves and the *alcheringa*. Enveloped in its coils, we soon feel what it is like to discriminate one from another because the *alcheringa* is a divine state peopled by all the Sky Heroes who made the world we know.

Thus, in a cave at Mootwingee, the image of the Rainbow Snake on the wall offers me a chance to meditate on the wonder of existence, knowing that if we allow its memory to die we open the way for our own destruction. Sacrificing the wildness within us on the altar of exploitation and waste is to erase forever our kinship with nature. When that happens, I know it is only a matter of time before the spirit of the *alcheringa* will rise up and erase *us* from the face of the earth.

Your friend

NOTES
1. Bill Neidjie, *Kakadu Man*, Resources Managers, Darwin, Australia, 1986.
2. Ibid.
3. Genesis 9:12–17.

SEVEN

ON THE
SACRED DRUM

Dear friend,

Let me tell you what lies before me on the table in my
room. A bell-shaped seed pod, no bigger than a coffee cup,
which serves as reminder to me of a remarkable man that
I met here on the island of Waiben. The pod belongs to
Wasikor, the sacred drum of Mer, one of the many islands
that happen to lie among the wave-washed atolls of Torres
Strait. How it came into my possession is a story that I
wish to relate, since by doing so I hope to unveil one of the
great mysteries that pertain to the man they call a *zogo le*.

My nomad friends advised me to make the short voyage
from the mainland to Waiben. It was suggested that if on
my travels I were fortunate enough to meet a *zogo le*, or
man of power, my understanding of the wild state would
be deepened considerably. Of course, I was not prepared

to make that judgement in advance, preferring to allow my inherent reserve in such matters to act as a brake. How was I to know whether an encounter with a *zogo le* might result in the acquisition of knowledge as my friends so naturally assumed? From past experience I knew they observed reality from a different perspective, so it was necessary for me to be sure our visions concurred.

But first I must enlighten you on the special nature which constitutes a *zogo le*'s most important attribute. He is one of those men, found only rarely today among the islands, whose high learning is inseparable from a deep knowledge of the spirit and of morality. In the Middle East such men are known as *orafä* and are regarded with reverence by all those who meet them. Their task is to act as the perfect sage, accumulating philosophic knowledge and spiritual experience, which in turn they are able to hand on to men who are eager to learn. In a sense, they are mystical philosophers, custodians of a sacred law without which the islanders would be lost. The *zogo le* is, like his *orafä* counterpart, an ornament of culture, a man who prefers to live anonymously and in the company of like-minded individuals.

Now you might say that such a fraternity is the product of an unstable constitution. Men who gather to speak of the wind and its power to create life have only themselves to blame when they discover the role of isobars in the conduct of weather patterns. But I can tell you now the *zogo le* dismisses such knowledge as superficial, knowing as he does that it takes no account of what he deems to be truly important. You see, he recognises that the soul's claims on the flesh are extreme. The wind he speaks of is not the wind that fills sails, but the wind which Rilke spoke of when he wrote, 'Oh, there's Night, there's Night, when wind full of cosmic space feeds on our faces . . .' The wind is designed to keep us on the alert, carrying us forward to our limits and beyond our limits.

So I crossed the strait and landed on Waiben. This small island outpost which had once been a prosperous pearl-diving haven has become a sleepy backwater since the advent of plastic. Pearl shell was an important commodity in the days when buttons were still made from natural substances. Men in helmets dived to great depths to wander the sea floor in search of this shiny nacre. Escorted by giant manta rays and sharks, they would send out bubbles as they gasped the air pumped from above. They too were in the grip of an invisible wind, the wind whose silence I was soon to learn we can only admonish with the sound of a sacred drum.

Though I am on an island, I feel at times as if I have quit the face of the earth! What abounds in the bay is flotsam, coconut fronds, empty shells spotted like leopards, warring gulls, and crabs that taunt the tides with their scavenging habits. The world of the sea is unlike any other. For someone such as myself who is familiar with the sound of his footfalls among bracken in the bush, sand offers a shifting platform, forever changing as the waves wash smooth one's momentary imprint. It is as if I had never been! My sensibility is marked only by its discontinuity. Knowing as I do that I am on the edge of things, I feel a sort of rapture as I walk upon this sandbar of solitude. I feel brave. Perhaps it is because I am beginning to savour in nature an abandon that previously I had never noticed.

But enough of this! Waiben offered me the community of men. The rambling hotel on the waterfront where I stayed reminded me of one of Somerset Maugham's old haunts when he, too, was a wanderer. An air of decayed

grandeur permeated the unpainted timbers on the verandah. Patched sofas and long-stemmed ashtrays in the
lounge reflected a time when the monthly packet boat
brought news from the south in the form of newspapers
and serial novels. From the verandah I could see the mainland in the distance. Outrigger canoes dipped at their
moorings. On the foreshore palms rustled in the wind.
Long sticks, known as *waps*, stood upright in the sand. I
soon discovered that these were harpoons used for spear-
ing dugong, a creature that, from all reports, appeared to
be a cross between a porpoise and a whale. Clearly, nature
had got its genetic wires crossed somehow as the dugong
lives a lonely life, conscious that it is neither fish nor fowl.

My companions at the hotel were the type one expects
to find in such a remote place. Solitude they wore like a
scar on their bare chests, close to the heart. No histories
were exchanged for fear of disrupting the unquestioning
silence. I concluded that each of us was burdened with a
secret which made it impossible to be ourselves. We were
victims of a knowledge so dangerous that it threatened to
destroy us. This deep well of consciousness into which we
had flung ourselves in the hope of quenching our thirst
was, in reality, a soak poisoned by too much introspection.
We had grown to prefer isolation as a means whereby we
could escape the need to *confront* one another. No wonder
the hotel had seen better days; when pearl was the object
of a man's endeavour, Lady Luck became a singular visi-
tant. In her arms men allowed themselves to be ravished
by an embrace made more tantalising by the knowledge
that the good Lady's charms might be withdrawn at any
moment.

Of course, this has nothing to do with *zogo les* or sacred
drums. But if you understand my state of mind at the time,

it will be easier for you to appreciate subsequent events. In my loneliness I was drawn to a dance festival in a public park near the beach. There a group of island children had agreed to perform for the benefit of their parents. I happened to sit by an elderly gentleman whose grey beard contrasted strongly with the dark colour of his skin. When the first dance ended, however, he made no attempt to applaud. Instead he appeared unmoved by what he had witnessed. When I remarked to him that the youths of his tribe had performed well, given their inexperience, he shook his head. He informed me then of the sadness he felt at watching one of his tribal dances enacted by uninitiated children.

You see, this man was conscious of the danger which can arise when events are *desacralised*. In his opinion the children of his village were not privy to the esoteric knowledge that made the dance a ritual enactment. Performance without any understanding of the hidden meaning meant the dance had been reduced to a mere husk in the interest of entertainment. As far as he was concerned only men who had been initiated and were privy to the symbolic nature of each movement of the dance could possibly do justice to what was wild and joyful in the instant itself. To him, each dancer must be akin to a flame, leaping forth from matter into ether, drunk with the denial of unreality. Only in the dance can a man trample on what is untrue and joyously destroy the very place upon which he stands. The opportunity of becoming intoxicated by the excess of change was to him the very essence of the dance. Wrestling with the spirit within the context of ritually prescribed movements meant he could vie in speed and variety with his own soul!

Was this a casual conversation on the edge of a clearing

under a plaited awning made from palm leaves, perhaps?
Not a bit of it. This man, Nagali, informed me that he was
from the crocodile totem, which meant he identified with
the creature as Toby Kangale did with the sea eagle. At
first, I took him to be someone who had allowed himself to
become a victim of disillusionment, until I realised his observations were made in response to his fears that his people were beginning to abandon the sea which made them.
Furthermore, Nagali confided in me that he was a *zogo le*,
a man of power, and a spiritual custodian of his people.
You can imagine my surprise when confronted with this
information. He reminded me of the wanderer Hayy ibn
Yaqzan from Avicenna's recital,[1] I had encountered a man
who, like the *pîr* of his story, could say:

> My name is *Vivens;* my lineage, *filius Vigilantis;* as to my
> country, it is the Celestial Jerusalem. My profession is to be
> forever journeying, to travel about the universe so that I
> may know all the conditions. My face is turned towards my
> father, and my father is *Vigilans.* From him I have learned
> all science, he has given me the keys to every kind of
> knowledge. He has shown me the roads to follow to the
> extreme confines of the universe, so that since my journey
> embraces the whole circle of it, it is as if all the horizons of
> all climes were brought together before me.

I can tell you, dear friend, there are times when a person
is grateful for the opportunity to meet a man of Nagali's
honesty and wisdom. Of course, I had heard such men do
exist, but I had always assumed their ilk inhabited the
mountains of Tibet or the forests of India. Yet here, on this
remote island among swirling tides, seashells, and hidden
reefs, I had encountered a man who understood what it
was like to be a *kerub* (cherub)—that is, a man who has

freed himself from the shackles of his body in order to embrace a life of knowledge. His discontent, moreover, was philosophic rather than personal. Indeed, his greatest concern was for the well-being of his people as they increasingly succumbed to the lure the mainland offered them in the form of casual trinkets dreamt up by advertising executives.

During our conversation, Nagali introduced me to many things. He spoke of his people in the days before white men had invaded their islands. He told me how they used to hunt dugong offshore, sometimes spending days at sea in their canoes. He informed me how they relied on the stars at night for guidance and the taste of sea water in the daytime. It appeared that a true connoisseur of the ocean could sip his way from island to island! In fact, Nagali insisted that a master navigator was a man capable of recognising a number of levels to his craft. Knowledge of practical details led in time to the attainment of a correct or 'moral' approach to his task. Attainment of a third level, however, meant that a master navigator was custodian of an esoteric knowledge. This knowledge implied his mind was 'filled with the sea' and that he had learnt to 'breathe with his feet'. Nagali inferred that a navigator must attune his breathing to the ocean swell, inhaling and exhaling 'all the way to his feet' as the canoe rises and falls. In so doing, his mind enters into communion with the sea to the point where he accepts the Lord of the Waves' body as his own.[2]

I know you are wedded to the security that charts and sextant offer when it comes to setting a course at sea. What you must understand is that Nagali was not telling me these things for any other reason than to ensure my collaboration. He wanted me to recognise that the soul of his people was embedded in an ancient aquarian tradition. As far as he is concerned, Wasikor, the sacred drum of Mer, merely echoed the sound the sea makes when it laps against the hull of a canoe bent on rediscovering the spirit of his people. So you see, the voyage he suggested I make with him was one of two people committed to a great undertaking. In our case, the undertaking was to recapture the spirit of his people's tradition in order to understand how they might have dealt with the problems of our present age.

Imagine the two of us sitting in the shade while island women in the clearing beyond sang old songs. Such was the intensity of our discussion we hardly noticed the sun slipping into the lagoon, a hot orb whose last light rekindled the cloud. Recalling memories of his youth in the company of his father, another *zogo le*, Nagali grew more animated, more entranced by the vivacity of the moment. I suspect he saw in me someone to whom he might unburden himself of the disappointment and regret that dragged like a sea anchor at his soul. You see, Nagali was conscious that the *zogo* to which he was heir was in danger of being lost. The reasons were indifference, the flaccidity of spirit that is born from a certain hardening of the heart, and the knowledge that the young people, at a time when they were most vulnerable to the teachings of men such as himself, were no longer being encouraged to sit at his feet and learn. Like an abandoned wreck, Nagali lay marooned on a reef, his knowledge being swamped and lost with each passing storm. What he knew of the old ways, the law, his people now considered to be little more than flotsam as they contemplated their government pension cheques and the thought of what they could buy.

I confess I was at a loss how to advise my new friend. He was talking of a condition vital to us all. The demise of ritual and traditional knowledge is bad enough; but when the flower of spiritual knowledge is denuded of its blooms, life's garden becomes a prey to weeds. True philosophers like Nagali and the *orafä* of the East rely on this paradisiacal garden for their survival. They know that without spiritual knowledge rooted in the subsoil of our lives we are lost. As husbandmen of the spirit they recognise how important it is to nurture the sacramental element, to ensure our deepening awareness, and understanding, of what is veiled. Knowledge of what is 'hidden' lends a flavour, a perfume to a man's life that lingers long after his absence has been noticed. He bears on his face a princely countenance in keeping with his regal stature as a descendant of the Lord of the Waves. Unfortunately, in Nagali's case, his tutelary role had all but been drowned under the wash of videos shipped in from the mainland.

My dilemma was acute. I had come to Waiben at the suggestion of my friends to meet with a *zogo le*. In turn, Nagali had made me aware of the dangers we confront when we are attracted by the facile radiance of all things modern. In the clearing beyond we had watched children perform a dance emptied of its meaning because they had been encouraged to dismiss its true spirit in favour of its effect. The days when a hunter asked forgiveness of a dugong as he harpooned it were over. The spirit-talk a man inhaled on the wind had been reduced to a conch shell of vague echoes. Nagali was a man alone, a castaway on an island, a Crusoe who had made solitude his boon companion. Until my arrival he had not thought to look on the beach for the footprints of another such as himself. He had become, in a sense, a cannibal, eating the 'skull, flesh, bones and whatever remain'd' of himself. The *zogo* his forefathers used to consume, when they ate the flesh of those they had killed in battle, Nagali now sought in an act of self-cannibalism. His tragedy was that he had become a casualty of our desire to eliminate from the memories of men the wild wind that made us.

You laugh at my apocalyptic pronouncements? The world cannot end, you say, since history goes on, an exterior event, not concerned with the end of the world. How can we worry ourselves over one *zogo le* who is unable to give up his reliance on myth and its esoteric significance? We who have abandoned the quill in favour of the word processor understand more than most the transience of the moment. By desacralising history we have at last made sense of it, since we now comprehend where we are going. Nowhere, if the truth be known! The siren of progress is luring us to our destruction just as surely as many of us are unable to find answers to the despair we suffer. What I suggest strikes at the very heart of our modern existence. To *give up* progress smacks of the mentality of lemmings that prefer death at the cliff edge than life on the plain. Yet, I ask you: are we not like lemmings if we fall headlong into an abyss of our own making? In reality the progress we identify with today represents a *denudation* of the spirit more far-reaching than any Nagali might experience. He suffers because of the loss of his traditions; we, unfortunately, no longer know what the word means.

Some *kerub*, you say! I talk of a vanished humanity at a time when the world is overpopulated. Better a few die of a broken spirit so that others may take their place. People occupy space, it is true; but I am more concerned with the vacuum our minds occupy in the wake of our love-affair with the modern condition than with any population explosion. In any event, the devastating effect of this explosion comes as a result of our refusal to entertain the idea of *restraint*—that is, to consider the alternative of non-action. We have become obsessed with activity at the expense of the meditative moment. Because of this we have reconstructed the sacred landscape of our forebears with our own selective parodies: nuclear reactors, sludge-filled rivers, cities crowded with skyscrapers, wild terrain cemented hard under highways, conveyor belts laden with useless products, fowls in battery cages enslaved to productivity, luxuries falsely advertised as enhancements to our well-being, airports pressed with people desperate to escape on holiday, the ugliness of our environment as we seek to modify it in accordance with our own bad taste. These are some of the images of our culture with which we surround ourselves. Can we justify our modern existence as the best of all possible worlds? Dear friend, is this the world we truly wish to impose on Nagali's people? If we do, then there is little that differentiates us from the Mongol hordes of old, because what we encounter we destroy with the same cruelty as they did with their swords.

What I speak of goes to the root of the modern crisis. We are in despair because we have lost all understanding of the sacred. Nagali despairs because he can see the same loss entering into the spirit of his people. Our friendship, however, had given him new hope for the future. Suddenly he could see he was not alone; that there were others in the world who feared for a future without spiritual knowledge of which he was custodian. I informed him that since we were *orafä* in spirit, our task was to ensure this knowledge assumed its rightful place as the true arbiter of men's souls.

It was then, in the gathering dusk, I first heard the sound of a drum. Its reverberation caught me by surprise since the sound came from the beach, not the clearing where we sat. When I enquired of Nagali as to the significance of this noise, he informed me we were hearing the voice of Wasikor, the sacred drum of Mer, rendering a lament. Upon whose death? I asked. Nagali replied that Wasikor's bride, Nimau, had fallen victim to the crew of a European ship one hundred years before. They had captured her and taken her away, probably to some museum in England. Since then Wasikor no longer played songs of courage and bravery; all he could do was mourn the loss of his wife. This, too, was why the drum chose the anonymity of the beach at night rather than present its fallen countenance to a people who had no power to bring Nimau back. Nagali admitted he was, like Wasikor, a drum without an echo, a man whose bride had been torn from him at a time when their lives had been most intertwined, like coral on the sea floor. Love, the Lord of the Waves' gift of eternity to all men, had been taken from him just as Wasikor had lost his spouse.

Later, when the drum ceased playing at the end of the evening, I accompanied Nagali down to the beach. He wanted to introduce me to Wasikor before the drum returned to its haven in another part of the island. You see, Wasikor was a loner, a singular drum whose dialogue with the wind was designed to combat any solicitations of doubt. According to Nagali, such a dialogue ensures that the demands our soul makes on our flesh keeps us breathless.

We discovered Wasikor in the lap of an old man, a friend of Nagali's, who was sitting under a palm on the edge of the lagoon. This man, Tabau, who was of the seagull totem, touched his breast and bowed his head as we approached. We sat beside him in the sand and, for a time, no words were spoken. Nagali wished me to gather in the image of Wasikor lying there in Tabau's lap. With an open jaw at one end and a tympanum made of skin at the other, Wasikor reminded me of a wounded bird whose wings had been broken by some brutal blow made by an unknown assailant. I felt sorry for this drum whose only repertoire now was made up of laments. Attached to its length were a number of small seed pods which rattled softly whenever Wasikor was moved. The sound they made was like that of small waves on the beach at tide turn.

Nagali and Tabau spoke a few words in their island dialect before the latter reached over and tore away one of these pods. He gave it to Nagali who, in turn, presented it to me. Then he informed me this gift came from Wasikor as a memento of our meeting. When I remonstrated that the pod was a part of Wasikor's *being* and that for me to accept it would be an act of sacrilege, Nagali replied that since Wasikor had been deprived of his spouse, my task was to travel the world in search of Nimau on his behalf. Wasikor's small echo of the waves was to be my talisman, linking me to the sacred voice of the drum itself. Furthermore, Nagali informed me, if one day I was fortunate enough to find Nimau, then the pod would act as proof of my identity. I was to bring Wasikor's bride back home to these islands so they might once more play together the songs of their people.

I was deeply touched by this display of trust. Nagali and Tabau had made me a *zogo le* like themselves. Wasikor, the lonely drum of Mer, was their voice. Listening to its plaint earlier, it occurred to me I had been made a cohort of theirs in the task of rebuilding the world. The sound of the sea and the murmur of the wind were entreating me by way of this drum. No wonder I regard the small seed pod on my table as a sacred object. It reminds me of what we all must do if we are to survive in the world. Find Nimau, the true femininity of spirit which we have allowed to be stolen from us, and return her to the arms of her husband.

Your friend

NOTES

1. Henry Corbin, *Avicenna and the Visionary Recital*, Spring Publications, 1980.

2. For further information see the article, 'Of Metaphysics and Polynesian Navigation' by James Barr, *Avaloka*, Vol. III, Nos. 1 & 2, Grand Rapids, 1989.

EIGHT

ON
WALKABOUT

Dear friend,

Let me tell you about a tree under which I slept last night. The baobab is like no other. Squat, bulbous, a smooth-trunked impresario with a penchant for accumulating water in the dry months, this tree drops velvet-skinned pods as large as a man's fist. To awake in the morning to the sight of such small hemispheres littering the earth is to know one has been visited by Mimi Spirits. These are their baubles, and the seed within them a clamour of echoes that suggest a fecundity not always visible.

Mimi Spirits, you say? Well, how else am I to describe a visitation by what is eternal? The baobab, after all, is a giant lingam, a phallus, filled with seminal substance. Leaning against its curvaceous trunk, it's easy to regard these pods before me as the playthings of spirits. More

than once I have seen them on cave walls in the arms of
Mimi figures, ochrous gourds which, when emptied, become ideal water carriers. Thus a man or spirit can journey
afar in search of verities, knowing that in his pursuit of
knowledge he will not die of thirst.

Is this possible? My friend, Idumdum, seems to think
so. He has made many journeys in the footsteps of his
forefathers during his lifetime, hoping to encounter their
lingering presence among the rocks and caves of the region. When he asked me to accompany him on a seasonal
visit to his country, I knew the privilege he wished to
bestow upon me was one of collusion. You see, Idumdum
had recognised in me a water carrier like himself. We were
creatures of the baobab, seed bearers, men who longed to
render what we saw and experienced as something more
than temporal.

So what I want to speak of now is the Dream Journey.
Idumdum has joined me in an excursion into the *alcheringa*. Much of what we have seen so far has a quality of
revelation, in keeping with the idea that we have, in a
sense, left the earth. By this I don't mean we are victims of
hallucination, nor are we candidates for the asylum! But it
is clear to me the elderly Wardaman tribesman knew when
he asked me along that we were to embark upon no ordinary journey. As far as he was concerned, he was taking
me to an *imaginary* place; a place that mirrored an ideal
state rather than any corporeal condition with which we
were familiar. His country, I soon realised, was none other
than a *spiritual universe* containing images supremely important to his well-being.

Our Copernican obsessions which fix the 'central fire' of
the sun at the centre of our universe preclude any dabbling
in the realm of the unseen. Gravitational forces, though

invisible, are felt, after all. We know they exist by the power of repercussion. In other words, what goes up must come down! Talking of an imaginary place in the realm of the actual smacks of sorcery and a desire to transcend reality. But is not the security born from the possession of an insurance policy any less an act of sorcery? The mind is 'set at rest', so to speak, when we know our lives and our property are insured. We have materialised security with the aid of actuarial arithmetic designed to neutralise the workings of chance. And chance, as we all know, is the consort of *risk*, one of nature's marriages of inconvenience which has bedevilled us with offspring we abhor. Who wants to encounter change, failure, dispossession in a world governed by the houris of success? These facile nymphs woo us with so-called real objects rather than with those that are invisible. This world, my dear friend, is what Idumdum has asked me to walk *away* from as we journey into the realm of the *alcheringa*.

All right, so I am talking about pilgrimage. Journeying to a far place in return for a cockle shell or a palm leaf. Souvenirs make the trip worth-while since they conjure up what was absent in the first place. What is so different from travelling to Santiago de Compostela or Jerusalem to visiting the *alcheringa* in the company of a Virgilian guide like Idumdum? He alone decides how far into the imaginal realm he wishes us to go. Saints' bones and those of his ancestors commingle in reliquaries and rock cavities just as surely as if they were of the same body. For a man, in death, assumes a transcendent mantle in keeping with the gods when his bones are cherished. It is for this reason we speak in hushed tones when we come upon a funeral platform in a tree. We know the bones above are destined for a new life as objects of *veneration* far in excess of that which they received in life. This is death's mystery: the loss of life can lead to a new, more rarified existence in the memory of others.

But enough of this. Idumdum's Dream Journey did conform to boundaries. For some days we have been travelling across country whose countenance features clumps of pandanus trees and tawny dead grass. In the dry season greenness announces itself more as a cameo than as a broad backdrop of succulence. Of course, birds followed us, particularly crows. Their tired caws reminded me of the sound of a most muted anguish, burdened as they are with the prospect of loss. They were indeed the voices of the dead, summoning us to put aside our fears and journey further into the hinterland of our own hearts. You see, a Dream Journey offers us the chance to travel *beyond ourselves*. No man knows for certain what lies at the end of such a journey until he has arrived. The fear we experience comes from a lack of trust rather than from any dangers that might lie in wait for us.

Thus in this tropical wilderness I am at the mercy of all that is omnivorous. Why, even as I awoke this morning, I sensed I was about to become a meal for ants! Nothing alive remains impervious to the process of digestion in one form or another. A train of bull ants marching in soldierly formation across the clearing signalled the beginning of my demise, had I remained to offer myself on their earthy salver. Instead I flicked them from my blanket—these horny insects whose bite bore with it a real threat of pain. Unlike the scarab beetle, I had no desire to imprison my spirit in a cocoon made from sheep dung and bodily secretions in order to protect myself. That would have meant I was afraid. Of what, you ask? Time, of course.

Nevertheless, this part of Northern Australia has its own

way of offering us a glimpse of the eternal. Craggy rock outcrops, shady gullies, mesas of grassland which give off an air of hidden valleys, large parrots that glide low through the underbrush, screeching like shades. On foot one is conscious of primeval dimensions that far outweigh any geological interpretation. A tree snake hanging from a branch raises its head, projecting the ancient uraeus on the forehead of pharaohs. A forked branch, broken away from a tree, reminds me of the *uas*, Egypt's paradoxical symbol of the marvellous act of creation and of the evil in existence. After all, have we not entered the realm of *Duat*, the netherworld, the place where truth is revealed?

According to Idumdum, we are approaching the land of the Lightning Brothers. Sanctuaries dedicated to their memory lie among the caves and cliff overhangs deep in the valley. Already I hear the voices of his ancestors singing songs that celebrate the feats of these warring brothers. For, it is told, they fought one another to the death over the wife of one of them. Yagjagbula was attracted to Ganayanda when Jabiringi was out hunting kangaroo one day. They eloped. When Rain began to fall, the Lightning Brothers flashed across the dark sky, destroying trees whenever they landed blows. Frogs watched and croaked. Such was the ferocity of their encounter that rocks split, causing springs to well forth from the ground. At Ngalanjari (Waterrock Dreaming) the two brothers are commemorated in ochre and pipeclay, their lengthy phalluses a testimony to their seminal power, their *paraunda*, in impregnating the earth. Their heads, aureoled with rays of the sun and one protruding horn, suggest majesty and the regal power of reconciliation as they struggle to resolve their cosmic dilemma. Ganayanda, Earth Mother that she is, must be fertilised by the supreme waters; it's up to them to merge their respective potencies into a more vital force to satisfy her demands.

When you make a Dream Journey there is always the hope that you will transcend yourself. Of course, this on-rush of intuition, this opening of the heart and mind to the special vibrations emanating from the earth, could suggest a willingness to remain shackled by instinct. But is this so wrong? Surely, to be impelled by what is innate supposes a desire to remain true to oneself. Turning away from one's origins—those giant phalluses that penetrate our psyche even as we might wish to dismiss their *paraunda*—will this make permanent the illusion of mastery that we currently enjoy? I doubt it. What people forget as they gaze out at the pollutant haze from their high-rise apartments is that the bite of *urbicus* is more poisonous than any tree snake. We moderns are killing not only ourselves but all life in our unthinking allegiance to rationality and progress. The rational mind calculates, measures, indeed adores the heady realm of quantifiable relationships. Whoever heard of nature burdening its primordial gaze with the weighty computations of the abacus? While Pythagoras may have informed us that nature was a mathematician, the numbers he was concerned with were *celestial*, not material. As a result, pure Euclidian space has been reduced to tenement blocks on the outskirts of cities, each one vying for the warming glance of sunlight on winter days.

My friend, history may be on the brink of collapse, not because of recent ideological agreement between super powers but because of our slavish abuse of the world in which we live. We have made eunuchs of the Lightning Brothers because we desire to control procreation rather than worship its tenets. Idumdum's icons have become flaking images in the eyes of those who reject all contact with the instinctive. Their vacant gazes remind us of an age when we were beholden to *growth*, not to the empty shell of productivity in which obsolescence shelters like a hermit crab. When I say that history is under siege, I mean that it has become the servant of man's desire to deify himself. By celebrating his own achievements at the expense of the divine, modern man displays an impulse to record events that becomes more important than the *meaning* of the event itself. The withdrawal of the gods from our everyday lives is our own doing, not theirs. They know when they are not wanted. They know also when the art of prophecy among men is dying.

Etymologically, the word history derives its source from the Greek for 'tissue' or 'web'. It also spreads its tentacles to the root verb 'to know'. Knowledge, wisdom, and the power to discern the truth are thus inherent in the meaning. The concept is imbedded in the idea of drawing knowledge together so that it forms a pattern of truth. This pattern, however, should not be seen as solely the preserve of man's preoccupation with his own past, but with the origin of all nature. Is not history written in tectonic striations where the earth's crust is detonated from below? Are not the withered wings of an emu a record of this bird's dismissal of flight? Doesn't a kangaroo's pouch denote a preplacental age when nature delighted in physiological experiment? What I am trying to say is, we must give up our belief in the idea that history is centred on *our* relationship to the world. This is what the story of the Lightning Brothers is telling us. The Mimi Spirits discourse among themselves. You can hear them between bars in a song. They relate a divine history equally as important to the web of knowledge as our own understanding of the forces within nature. A cyclonic disturbance has equal right to be viewed in terms of a mythical encounter as a meteorological event. Imagine how rich the weather report might be if we heard it as a chronicle of gods at odds with themselves!

You accuse me of jest? Or see me as some arch-trickster of the *alcheringa?* Dear friend, listen to your own heart. Discard all that modern debris you have clung to for so long and swim towards me, the wing-heeled figure who taunts you from afar. The wild state demands a certain kind of attitude. Hiding behind pinstripes, the ordered expanse of collar and tie, actually *separates* us from what terrifies. And yet, when we are afraid, are we not most alive? Do we not confront, at last, the wide belly of the whale when we have abandoned ourselves to the waves? The story of Jonah or Markandeya, the ancient Hindu sage, tells us as much. Living in the stomach of the all-containing god, Vishnu, Markandeya inadvertently falls out of his mouth into life. There he experiences the idea of Maya, illusion, a condition which until then he had not experienced. Living inside a god he had known only a reality congenial to his nature. But outside, in the world of duality, Markandeya realised what he had considered complete and ordered was in fact little more than a mirage. Vishnu had deliberately opened his mouth to allow him to escape from the primordial condition. He had wanted him to experience the limits of individualised consciousness before returning to the unfragmented world of his, the god's interiority. Vishnu knew Markandeya must suffer, must know how irreconcilable Maya really is, before he could hope to attain to that worshipful silence known only to the true sage.

I think this is why Idumdum has brought me along on his Dream Journey. It's hard enough for my nomad friends to bridge the conceptual gap lying between them and people like ourselves. While we are content to revel in abstractions rather than in life, they know they must fall from the mouth of the god occasionally if they are ever going to return to the *alcheringa* at death. I am sure, for Idumdum, the land we walk upon represents Maya. He revels in its beauty and the mysterious silence it offers; but equally, he is aware that to transcend its illusory power, he must transcend himself. For this reason, his country becomes an imaginary experience, the belly of a god, wherein he is able mentally to reconstruct paradise and so keep company with Mimi Spirits.

Idumdum and his friends regard the earth, their land, as a celestial image. They are enamoured by its many categories of sacredness. For these possess their souls, transforming their habitat into the vision of an ideal iconography. In the presence of the Lightning Brothers everything is transfigured to the point where this new intensity lights up their own lives, endowing them with a victorious and supernatural strength, which consecrates them as beings of the *alcheringa,* clothed as they are in that special hieratical dignity known as *paraunda.* This is the imaginal land of their ancestors, those men and women who saw the earth not as a dead thing, but as an icon capable of reflecting the outer and the inner world.

Making the earth a fetish calls into question the supreme relevance of science. In factories and steelworks facile alchemies are performed each day that bely the sanctity of earth. The Lightning Brothers' phalluses are no match for the imperturbable muscle of science. Dear friend, have you not looked out of your window of late? I mean, with a heart not yet inured to the way anguish manifests itself? The pain of observing man's inhumanity to himself in a picture from Auschwitz is readily duplicated in any industrial landscape today. The earth suppurates under oil slicks, poisonous chemicals, gases, industrial waste, sewage, and the foul refuse of our modern existence. We have made the earth, which we rely on to survive, a dumping ground for all we no longer have need of. Crime, drug addiction, mental disorder, abandoned children bewildered by the earth's destruction, and an endless legislature of laws that further govern our every move—these constitute the whirlwind we reap in our pursuit of plenty and the so-called benefits of modern existence. At our death we do not leave behind sackcloth, a few household items, and the memory of a thousand meals eaten in the shade of olive groves. Instead, our legacy is innumerable tons of irreducible waste, and the knowledge that we have been passive appendages to the body-manufact. Compliant consumers most of us, we have made of our bodies a massive garbage dump which we delight in filling. Consumerism is the real canker eating away at our spirits. It seems as if we long to be wrapped in aluminum foil more than we do the healing power of the Lightning Brothers.

This is the crux of the matter. We have allowed ourselves to become victims of an obsessive desire for comfort. In so doing we have enslaved the earth, robbed it of its wild spirit. Under the banner of progress we have overexploited to the point of destruction the very things of which we're made, those four alchemical elements—earth, air, fire, and water. These now are languishing in furnaces, chemical mixtures, reactors, disposable products, carcinogenic compounds, and those ozonal predators that eat away at the atmosphere's protective layer. They live on as embittered exiles, condemned to support our exaggerated sense of what is required to survive. The hunter-gatherer in us has been killed off by the stock-market expert. The sage has succumbed to the economist. Wherever you look, you see an army of accountants totting up our right to exist within monetary guidelines. And the *celestial* account has been tossed aside because, according to the experts, the ineffable nature of the Lightning Brothers cannot be computed.

The basis of contemporary existence, is driven by the despicable logic of evolutionists and monetarists. Survival of the fittest, progress, growth, excess, market forces, restructuring, gross national product, fiscal management, debt repayment—this is the current jargon of today, the main language we are taught to understand. When Idumdum speaks of the bones of his forebears lying safely in rock clefts we are lost for words. Or we think of the possible market opportunity that exists out here for undertakers! We have allowed the language of materialism to drown out the last echo of the inner chorus we once knew by heart. The song denoting our *primal* concerns has been submerged under the wash of blasphemies that masquerade as our reason for existence. We have allowed ourselves to become lifelong victims of an economic rather than a spiritual process. In so doing we have adopted the illusion that the raucous sounds of satiety are an acceptable substitute for the music of the spheres.

But, out here in Idumdum's country, we are confronted with another reality altogether. The Lightning Brothers are our celestial guides of the *alcheringa*. Nearby, the bones of Idumdum's father and relatives lie in rock cavities, small bundles of numen that spell continuity for a short time only, given that the earth is always changing. But Idumdum is content. He recognises in the empty gaze of his father's skull much more than the 'noble dust of Alexan-

der' which, according to Hamlet, merely threatens to stop
a bung hole. He sees in it the object of his own Dream
Journey, a return to the place of his origin where the spirit
of his birth was first conceived. You see, a Dream Journey
is a way of coming to terms with our incompleteness, with
the noticing beast within ourselves. This animal in us is
aware of pain and sadness, of course; but it also knows
what we're moving towards is nearer than we imagine.
More tender perhaps as well. Each step we make into the
imaginal landscape of our being, whether it be filled with
ochrous hieroglyphs or a remnant of the wild nature which
first adored *us*, is, I now realise, a step in the right direc-
tion. The homeward journey is made up of an infinite
series of departures, all of which lead us towards the tomb.

The wheeling wedgetail eagle overhead signaled that we
had arrived. In the rock shelter Idumdum led me to where
I found myself in the presence of the Lightning Brothers
for the first time. They gazed at me with their sombre,
ambiguous eyes. Their giant phalluses seemed to be an
extension of their cerebral horns. Or were they the uraeus
on a pharoah's head? Why, each mouth and nose was
linked by a sacred snake! Now breath, word and procre-
ative member had become one. We were in the grip of the
seminal instant, the vigour of time transcended by the
paradox of myth. Indeed myth is *timeless*, the only instru-
ment we have to protect ourselves from death. For Idumdum, and for me also, the Lightning Brothers were a
perfect image of the eternal.

It was then Idumdum commenced to perform a strange
ritual. He walked over to a small incision at the end of
Yagjagbula's penis and began scraping it with a stick. As
he did so, he sang a song in the Wardaman dialect. His
expression was trance-like, remote, and it was clear he had

forgotten my presence. Only when he had completed the ceremony did he return to this world and begin to explain to me what had transpired. 'We need to cut Old Man Rain to make him bleed', was the way he explained it. I was given to understand in this masturbatory act the Lightning Brothers would be prevailed upon to embark upon a new cosmic battle. Rain, renewal, and the prospect of invoking the fecund spirit of the earth was the object of the ritual. Idumdum's task was to open the floodgates by his act of sympathetic magic.

I sat at the entrance to the cave and watched my friend. In the act of reverence towards his Dreaming ancestors he had shown me how important it is to engage in a dialogue with the gods. Their language makes no use of words, but they do manage to communicate a message more substantial than thought. Their comfortable signs fill apses, and the limbs of men begin to feel inexpressible joy each time the god-stone stirs them with its mysterious message. I could hear a murmur of the deep elements within myself. In the cave of the heart all the mornings of mankind were filled with birdsong. There is a mystical nexus between bones and stone that previously I had never observed. The former are the airy gift of the departed, their signatures; while the latter makes up their quintessence, the sacred substance so beloved of alchemists. No wonder I enjoy the confidence of Yagjagbula and Jabiringi nowadays; as avatars they have introduced me to my true nature. What I perceive now has all the hallmarks of spontaneity, and so my imagination is in the process of being metamorphosed.

Your friend

NINE

ON THE
LIVING DEAD

Dear friend,

There is something unusually formal about a pile of bones lying at the entrance to a cave. Bundled like faggots, they absorb the night air with a luminosity born of absence. You see, the *birrimbirr* soul has departed. As a white cockatoo or smoke the spirit has risen to the clouds where it is transformed into rain. The bones that remain are no more than a vestige, a husk, of the man who has been. His *birrimbirr* soul has returned to the *alcheringa,* the Dreaming, where it is received into the vast reservoir of ancestral power that vivifies the land. In contrast his *mokuy* spirit—that is, a man's malign aspect—often stays around to trouble the living and to haunt the ground close to the dead man's heart. These two spirits, siblings of the afterlife, must be reconciled as protagonists if a man's soul is to be laid to rest.

I do not agree with you when you say that death is the chief subject of reflection for the living, and their chief care, when a people are surrounded by luxury, by acquisition and abundance. Such a viewpoint, I'm sure, stems from the boredom we moderns feel when we confront the prospect of our own demise. Since we have lost our sense of the afterlife, we find ourselves consumed by the object that has replaced it. Have you not heard of the void? This emptiness eats away at our hearts more than we care to admit. It is not so much that our anima departs at death, nor is it that our *birrimbirr* soul rises like some white bird to join the primordial waters; it is our failure to come to terms with the fact that we are metaphysical more than we are biological beings in origin.

My nomad friends understand the importance of reconciling these two aspects of their being. This is why they are at pains to perform elaborate mortuary rites whenever a tribal member dies. They are conscious that the *birrimbirr* and *mokuy* spirits must be reconciled before a man can truly be at rest with his ancestors. Not to perform these rites would be to condemn a man to a painful existence, separated from his ancestors, as a shade whose lingering presence causes birds to cease their twitter and crocodiles to slither down the bank to the seclusion of their pool. For all nature retreats in the wake of an unmortified soul. You see, the important thing about death for my friends is that they are able to distinguish it from dissolution. They know that a man dies *for* something, if he dies at all.

Why I speak of these things is that recently I had occasion to attend the funeral of a Yolngu child. The Yolngu live here in northeast Arnhem Land, on the edge of the Arafura Sea. Their lives are governed by the sea and the tribal land that backs onto the bay along the Gangan River.

Do you know, these tribesmen own salt water and fresh-water songs? I mean, they actually belong to them. I have never imagined a song to partake of a waterfall or a wave, have you? One salt water song I heard during the funeral ceremony told of the rising tide washing away footprints in the sand. Clearly, this song referred to the wiping away of all physical evidence of the dead child, just as the tide has the power to erase all trace of an earlier existence. Such songs constitute a map of the journey a soul must make to reach its destination. They remind the living of the journey they too must make one day when their time comes to die.

Narritjin, my Yolngu friend, informed me there was no obvious reason for the child's death. When they awoke one morning they found the infant dead in its crib. Nevertheless, it was incumbent on him to announce to all the outlying tribesmen that they must return to the encampment for the funeral. He did this by solemnly singing the song of the Guwak, an ancestral being, announcing the death over the radio transmitter. At no point did he acknowledge the dead child's name. This I concluded was to ensure that the *mokuy* spirit remained ignorant of what was about to occur. Narritjin had no wish to impede the escape of the *birrimbirr* at this critical time when no mortuary ceremony had been performed to protect it.

Try to imagine the strange air of discontinuity that pervaded the encampment as soon as the funeral was announced. All normal activity ceased. People wandered from one group to another, all the while speaking softly. Many women threw themselves on the ground and attempted to cut their heads. Those who were related to the dead child were forbidden to go near the coffin in case they encountered the *mokuy*. Some of the menfolk sang songs connected with places familiar to the child in life, in their attempt to say good-bye to the child's spirit. Throughout the day people arrived from the bush and joined their friends in the encampment. What I did not realise initially was that these songs were also being sung in order to bring people together before the ritual of painting the coffin commenced.

The coffin-painting began on the morning of the third day. Two young men in their middle twenties sat in the shade of the lean-to and ground out ochre and pipeclay. These men were regarded as experts. Their task was to give power to the body to aid it in its spirit journey. The paintings were considered to be important adjuncts— icons, if you like—said to invest the child's body with the special power of the ancestors. Without the paintings to accompany the child, his chances of reaching the realm of the Dreaming unscathed were considerably reduced. His *mokuy* would be out there somewhere, a malign and disruptive energy, waiting to grapple with his *birrimbirr* and so carry it off. Narritjin and other elders advised the painters on each element of the painting since the decoration belonged to the child's totem country. In this case the Freshwater Crayfish ancestor mingled with the floodwaters of the river. Together they encountered a fish trap used by the Sky Heroes to catch the crayfish. According to Narritjin, every man has built into his being at birth a set of paintings which must be expressed in life. Consequently, in death, a man's spirit must express these paintings also. So the ritual of coffin-painting is an essential element in the funeral process. In this case, the child's spirit's paintings become the decorative backdrop to his death. He goes towards the *alcheringa* clothed in the spotless archetype of himself, for these paintings do not address the senses but the spirit. Accordingly, they evoke the 'gladdening sorrow' of birth and death all in one motion of the artist's brush. Thus the child's coffin acts as a covenant between his *birrimbirr* and the realm of the Dreaming.

All this heady ceremony unnerved me at first. I kept imagining myself standing by the road watching a hearse cruise past, its black elongation fitfully flowered. A polished wooden coffin behind glass panels gives no indication of who is inside, as you know. A businessman or a bankrupt cannot be distinguished behind the brown patina of oakwood. No paintings, no *alcheringa* icons, no spotless existence are intimated in the chromed handles on either side. What I am witnessing is the presence of morbidity and *darkness*, the veiled and mechanised movement of a body to its final resting place. But here, on the edge of the Arafura Sea, I sense that there are other forces at work. When Yolngu people die, the journey they embark on is more taxing than the one our dead are expected to traverse *en route* to the graveyard across town.

Let me put it another way. The painted coffin is a veritable code of meaning expressing a man's relationship with his land and with the Dreaming. When the songs speak of wet season floodwaters surging down the inland rivers towards Gangan, we know the singer is expressing the *power* inherent in these waters to drag blackened tree trunks from muddy bottoms. In the same way it is hoped the *birrimbirr* of the deceased child will overcome obstacles and flow forward to its homeland at Gangan. The spirit of the child is not without guidance in its wanderings, it seems, given that the coffin evokes the difficulties of the journey.

Soon afterwards, Narritjin and his friends began to perform the Yellow Ochre dance. The men had already painted their bodies with ochre and pipeclay, signifying their identification with the dance. Holding dilly bags in their mouths and digging sticks in their hands, they began by thrusting their sticks in the ground and moving them from side to side. In this way they reenacted the digging up of the sacred colours of the Dreaming in the *alcheringa* quarry site known as Gurunga. I was told later by Narritjin that yellow ochre represents the blood of the body. Just as a person digs up ochre and places it in a dilly bag, so men put it on their bodies. Opening the earth with the digging stick becomes a metaphor for opening up the coffin and the dead child's body. Putting the ochre in the dilly bag represents the act of placing the body in the coffin. So, yellow ochre is transformed in the same way that wine is in the Eucharist. Through an act of majesty an ordinary material element is identified with the blood of the sacred ancestors.

Can you imagine what this means? The power of the *mokuy* spirit is demeaned. What we know as the dark angel that stands at the foot of the bed while we are dying is confronted by the *birrimbirr* at the moment when its potency has been strengthened by a ritual act. The dancers make the spirit live! What the ancient Egyptians called the *Ka* bird is able to wing its way to its other self, the *Ba* bird of the *Duat*. Until this happens, until the *birrimbirr* meets up with its ancestral alter ego in the *alcheringa* (often identified as the meeting between two little birds, *chirchurkna* and *arumburinga* among certain nomad tribesmen) the deceased's soul is never truly free. The *mokuy* lays claim to it just as worms destroy mangrove trees, eating away at their trunks to the point where they collapse. It is the agony of this destruction that the living feel when they encounter the *mokuy* abroad on still afternoons. They know that someone's soul has not yet reached the *alcheringa* safely. Lost, and without purpose, it wanders among the paperbark trees, electrifying the air with its anguish. It is a chilling reminder of the importance of ritual if a man is to return to his spiritual hearth.

Death for us represents *cessation*, a material dissolution. A man's soul is no more than a mild electrical discharge that can be charted on a CAT scanner. There is no journey to the fabled Orient we can hope to make in pursuit of what Rimbaud called the 'first and eternal wisdom'. What we are left with instead is a dream of vulgar indolence! You and I are condemned to a *mokuy* life conscribed as it is by our modern wretchedness. The small *birrimbirr* within us no longer wrestles with the dark angel as of old because it is content to enter the void as a vague and unruly conscript. The anguish we feel, the anguish Rimbaud identified with the Occident, is the anguish of identifying too closely with this paradise of sadness that we know as modern life. Yet in spite of his spiritual apostasy Rimbaud did recognise that 'through the spirit we go to God'.[1] I ask you—was he not identifying with the *birrimbirr*'s journey to the *alcheringa?*

Journeying to the crocodile's nest involves us all in one way or another. The moment we paint our bodies with yellow ochre we become the living dead. When this happens my friends talk of entering into a state of *likan* which, translated literally, means 'elbow'. In common usage, it can also mean the junction point between a branch and the trunk of a tree. But, on another plane altogether, it can mean the link between the mundane and supramundane worlds, between the world of manifestation and the spiritual domain. Performing a ritual act beside the body of the deceased a man is *likan*—that is, he has set up a link between himself and the Dreaming.

The singing of numerous clan songs further encourages the child's *birrimbirr* to journey to important places associated with each member of his family and their ancestors. As Narritjin explained it to me, 'The child's spirit is going into each of the main places. That's why the singers follow the rule that the spirit should go from place to place when they sing. We all think this way when we're alive. When we're walking from place to place, we're already thinking of where we'd like to go when we die. So, when we do, it's important that our spirit journeys to our mother's place, or to our father's place. In this way we're sure we're still one mob, old friends with our ancestors'.[2]

It crossed my mind that my nomad friends are perpetually making *two* journeys. While they are walking from one *likan* place to another in daily life, they are also anticipating an interior journey to the *alcheringa* when they die. While they are journeying forward into youth, maturity and old age, they are also journeying *backward* into death, into a condition they associate with their origin. Clearly the *mokuy* and *birrimbirr* spirits are identified with these two excursions. The *mokuy* represents their appetite for life and their fear of death. No wonder it needs to be contained at the end. For these unappeased appetites to remain abroad without being reconciled creates a psychic disturbance among those that are living. Conversely, the *birrimbirr* spirit may be likened to the luz-bone, that kernel of immortality said to lie at the base of the spine, which is capable of being resuscitated in glory if the conditions are right. The *birrimbirr* is that scintilla of the Dreaming present in everyone. It is the fire of our ancestors glimmering in the cavern of our soul. The journey it makes back to the *alcheringa* is the journey all light makes back to its source.

The day of the interment—that is to say, when the coffin was to be buried in the crocodile's nest—dawned warm and humid. A breeze whipped up the sea, causing broken white caps off shore. Meanwhile the child's clan ancestor, Yellow Snake, was already swimming upstream, tasting the waters to see whether they were still salty. In so doing, it was rediscovering the child's spirit and swallowing it whole. As Narritjin remarked to me, 'If Yellow Snake feels that the water tastes good, then he drinks the box'. Drinks the box! To the rippling sound of clapsticks, signifying running water and the swallowing action of Yellow Snake, the child's spirit returns to the belly of the ancestral snake of his clan in this act of drinking the box.

At the same time, tassles fashioned from feathers and string are laid in the coffin. These ritual objects are usually made from long skeins of string unravelled at earlier ceremonies, and are often worn as part of a head-dress at circumcisions. Such an article inevitably gains power through its association with ritual events. This power, known as *madayan* by Narritjin's people, is considered sacred. To lay it in the coffin is to place in close contact with the body a manifestation of sacred law so that it is protected during the journey home to the *alcheringa*. Narritjin explained it thus:

> The tassle protects the body. We know that *madayan* comes from under the ground, from a deep place. That's why, as the body is going under the ground, we should send *madayan* with the body. *Madayan* lasts for ever, and protects the body for ever. So wherever the body goes it should always be with the *madayan*.

The child's body in its tiny coffin swims upstream, accompanied by ancestral snakes whose coils are supreme. We who pride ourselves on clandestine gestures when it comes to acknowledging death find it difficult to accept such visible ructions. Our bones are identified with worms, with decay, not with any interior voyage. After all, the land of our ancestors accounts for little when its conservation conflicts with our economic aims. This is why we so readily dig up its physical manifestation and ship it away to smelt in faraway places. Do you realise, my friend, we are destroying our birthright, our primordial heritage, each time we send trucks down into an open-cut mine? Indeed, we are no longer capable of seeing land as an *extension* of ourselves in the way that Narritjin and his people do. Thus we are unable to make a spirit journey back to our origins by way of primordial landmarks whose *likan* links us to our celestial origins.

We must confront this dilemma within ourselves. We can no longer condone the rape of nature to appease our apparently insatiable appetites. The world is finite and therefore exhaustible so long as we exploit it beyond its ability to renew itself. This is the environmental equation that we have yet to master: how to give back to the earth as much as we receive. Such a gesture is implicit in Narritjin's people's mortuary rituals performed at the death of the child. They know that the *whole* man must be aided in the return journey, not just his physical aspect. In contrast, we are so enamoured by our existence in the world that we have lost all sense of that metaphysical oasis known as the 'landscape of Xvarnah' in Mazdean theology. This is best described as an earthly landscape in which everything is transfigured by a scintilla of light which the soul projects onto it. In so doing, the soul is able to perceive the energy derived from this sacral light as the power that causes rivers to flow, plants to germinate, clouds to drift by, and people to be born. The energy further endows them with a victorious and supernatural strength which consecrates them as objects of religious dignity.

It is the symbolic process that the Yolngu people understand implicitly when they perform their mortuary rituals. They know they are 'giving back' to the earth not only their physical body, but also the sacred aspect of their beings which they identify with the *birrimbirr* spirit. In a way, the victory of *birrimbirr* over that of *mokuy* signifies the victory of the spirit over the purely venal, the metaphysical over the terrestrial. Until we understand—no, rediscover, the relationship between ourselves and the imaginal realm of the *alcheringa,* as Narritjin and his people do, then we will continue to desecrate the earth without being aware of the consequences in *non-material* terms. Science may bequeath to us appropriate checks and balances in due course, but even these will prove to be illusory and subject to degradation so long as the fundamental issue is not addressed. That is, each of us must reconstitute the landscape of the Dreaming (Xvarnah) in our hearts and minds rather than remain inhabitants of that paradise of sadness which we believe now to be inescapable.

My friend, perhaps this letter has proved to be a harrowing experience for you. Death is no pretty experience, especially when it is equated with the threatened destruction of our planet! But are not these synonymous? The whole world is precariously poised. The choice is ours whether we wish it to become a wasteland or not. I know of no more important issue facing mankind today. Re-establishing our link—our *likan*—with the realm of the Spirit is the only way we will ever be able to arrest the processes of self-annihilation that we are inflicting upon ourselves. If we do not heal the rift then we are doomed to a limited temporal life as *mokuy* spirits. And even that will end when we have exhausted all contact with the *birrimbirr* within ourselves.

When next you hear the shy chirping of the *chichurkna* bird in the undergrowth (or even on some street corner!), you will begin to listen! I know it is hard for you. Your computer screen arraigns you with its endless rows of figures, and the world beyond your window shudders under a great load of budget deficits and the threat of war. But I ask you to look beyond these abstract paradigms, which serve only to clutter the interior landscape that was once the preserve of angels. In us all there is a *birrimbirr* struggling to return to its source. Paint imaginal pictures of its *alcheringa* landscape on your own palpitating heart. Prepare your coffin for the voyage upstream in the company of Yellow Snake. Does the water still taste salty, perhaps? Remember, there are great chunks of knowledge lying on the bottom of the river, ready to be dislodged by a fast-flowing revelation of one sort or another.

My plea to you is not to look upon death as a finite end. All the great traditions concur when they affirm a continuing existence in the other world. Whether the condition is known as the Duat, Alcheringa, Bardo, Xvarnah, or Paradise, they all acknowledge that a voyage of return is involved. By dismissing the existence of the other world, are we not forsaking our vocation as travellers—as men who, when approaching strangers, are entitled to be known as *kat exochens*, or 'outstanding eminences'? In the minds of the Yolngu people, journeying to the *alcheringa* in a painted coffin makes one into an outstanding eminence. The temporal condition is discarded, and one is able to enter at last into the luminous realm inhabited by the ancestors.

Eventually, the child was carried to a grave in the nearby forest. Songs of the Mangrove Tree ancestor and the Mother Crocodile accompanied the dancers as people gathered around. Lowered into the hole at last, the coffin now contained the 'eggs' of the Mother Crocodile. A fire dance was performed to encourage the gestation of the eggs, thereby ensuring the child's spirit would be reborn in the *alcheringa*. The process of bringing the dead back to life, of making sure the child's *birrimbirr* reached its destination safely was now complete.

I think we were all relieved to know nothing had been left to chance, that the rites had been conducted in accordance with age-old practice. To know the dead child had transcended time and entered into a divine union at last, a sacred marriage with nature, meant we who are living would all benefit, I'm sure. In this respect, I only hope someone recalls the paintings that express my being when it comes to decorating *my* coffin, otherwise I'll end up as a *mokuy* spirit, wandering aimlessly among fern glades and termites' nests, looking for a way out of the maze.

Your friend

NOTES

1. Arthur Rimbaud, *A Season in Hell*, New Directions, translated by Louise Varèse, 1945.

2. Howard Morphy, *Journey to the Crocodile's Nest*, Australian Institute of Aboriginal Studies, Canberra, Australia, 1984.

TEN

ON SAND
SCULPTURE

Dear friend,

How moved I was to have received a letter from you at last. I had begun to suspect the distance which lies between us was made up of more than just space. In my enthusiasm for wildness as a philosophic premise, I wondered on occasions whether I might have alienated you more than your silence had begun to suggest. Were you brooding or did my discoveries upset the equilibrium to which your whole being is directed? Furthermore, I was afraid you might believe I had given up my allegiance to contemporary existence in the interest of espousing a more radical mode of thought. Well, in one sense you're right. In the words of Bill Neidjie, I have allowed feeling to make me, out here in open space.

I know this may come as a shock to you. A wide gap

separates those who dismiss dirt as inanimate waste, and those who regard it as a *power* that reminds them of their true origin. Yet we—that is, you and I—straddle a concept that is given over to the creation of waste out of what we clearly despise. By our industry we are wedded to the idea of generating wealth far in excess of our own limitations in order to aggrandize ourselves and show our supremacy over nature. The arithmetic is simple: we have grown to expect the environment to return to us with *interest* much more than we are prepared to give it in return. While we might regard monetary inflation as vaguely immoral, a symptom of declining values perhaps, we are less inclined to view nature's steady deflation in the wake of our ever increasing demands upon it as anything more than an aberration that can be arrested by science or technology.

I will confess to you, I am in a quandary. Out here in the wilderness I find myself drawn by an obscure force into confronting myself as someone whose rawness is real rather than contrived. Indeed, I now realise that a man requires intimate and solitary contact with wild places if he is to survive. When he is deprived of this state he begins to withdraw into himself, a prey to inner demons and the psychic wallpaper that passes for his estrangement from any genuine inner life. Since we have lost our thirst for limpidity, we have sought instead to invest our outward persona with all the heraldic mantling of modern life. The physical world has become our shield upon which we fashion all the augmentations of material well-being and status. In so doing we joust with the devil because we are wholly given over to the bliss of falling away from ourselves. As we face the end of yet another millennium, how many among us have the courage to demand an end to the pillage we have for so long condoned in the name of progress? I know I falter, since I fear the consequences of turning my back on all that supports me in my wants.

Is not this the dilemma that confronts all of us? And, conversely, one my friends have never considered because of the minimality of their existence? Their lives are so confined by place and organic functions that the extent of their world can be transcended only in an act of imaginative experience. They have no possibility of boarding an aircraft and flying off to a new environment as we do. Instead they must create their environment with all the power of *innocence* at their command. It is into nature they journey, singular wayfarers all of them, who are blessed with intellects untrammelled by any concept of material gain. They do not shudder at the loss of a divine sorrow as we do, for the Dreaming continues to nurture them with all the love of a mother. They lie in its embrace, succoured by immortality in the form of a ritual relationship with death.

Why I tell you these things is that recently I stumbled upon a sculpture made from sand here on the beach. Can you imagine what it was like for me to find myself surrounded by a series of abstract patterns which had been made by pushing up the sand into ridges? It appears my Yolngu friends had recently been engaged in a ritual known as the *Ngarra* ceremony. The sand sculpture, or *djel* (meaning 'surface of the earth') they had created reminded me of the kind of schema we might use to describe the internal organs of a woman. Here was the uterus, here the Fallopian tubes through which the fertilised egg descended from the ovaries. This impression of mine is purely arbitrary and has no basis in fact. But I know one thing: the purity of the design struck me as the product of extremely ordered minds. The men who had created the sculpture in the sand had a clear understanding of what they wished to portray. The *djel* was a complex mythological map detailing the voyage a man's spirit makes to the Dreaming at his death.

I was fascinated by the symmetry of these sand ridges. Nowhere before had I ever encountered such a careful execution of an image which was obviously derived from a different order of experience altogether. You see, the sand sculpture partook of something I could only assume was *sublime*. The journey that it explored reminded me of Dante's words when he remarked, 'I had set foot in that part of life beyond which one cannot go with any hope of returning'. Here, in the sand, was a striking physical resemblance to the great poet's trek up Mount Purgatory in his quest of paradise. How else can I describe to you the maze-like corridors, the feeling of *entry* that the *djel* conveyed? Indeed, I might have been mistaken in believing that what lay before me was the plan of a Sakkaran pyramid outside Memphis, with its narrow tunnels leading to the hallowed tomb of the mummy. My Yolngu friends had constructed a pure, geomantic design in keeping with some of the great mystical edifices of mankind. I was left with the inescapable conclusion these tribesmen were in possession of the archetype of all mystical edifices to which we are heirs. There seemed to be no accident that in each *djel* I subsequently viewed, the plan of Chartres, the Taj Mahal, Angkor Wat, even the sacred Egyptian hieroglyph itself, found its prototype. And when I later studied a sand sculpture, shaped by another clan member for a washing ceremony following the death of a friend, I knew I was looking at the emerging shape of the Egyptian hieroglyph *ankh*, meaning 'life'.

I have seen a sand sculpture for a smoke ceremony which is shaped like a Viking grave site. Another washing

ceremony *djel* I witnessed duplicated almost exactly a Byzantine cross from the cathedral of Cosenza. Such shapes in
the sand only made me realise I had stumbled among a
variety of configurations whose origins were metaphysical
rather than psychological. Like Dante, I had embarked
upon a journey from which there was no likelihood of
return. Each *djel* was the reflection of the spiritual *condition*
of the deceased, and served to ensure the journey his spirit
made was in accordance with his clan and totemic existence when alive.

Where does all this leave me, you may ask? In a state of
amazement, mostly! It's one thing to go for a walk along
the beach in search of solitude; quite another to find oneself surrounded by the hieratic moments in a man's inner
journey. We gaze in awe at tomb reliefs in Egypt, or mandalas in Tibet, depicting transitionary stages in the journey
of a departing soul for the other world, and of course
respect their hieratic dignity. How much more poignant it
is to discover these same icons laid out in the sand at your
feet by friends you know! And to think the tide will soon
wash them away and so erase what had earlier been an
inner experience. Clearly, the mind is neither so pure nor
so idolatrous that it can dismiss the walls of its tombs in an
act of transcendence. Otherwise what point is there in
ritually washing the body at the centre of one of these sand
sculptures?

But let me tell you what happens. The construction of
each sand sculpture is supervised by a clan member of the
deceased, known as an *anmari*. His task is to make sure the
design conforms to a strict ritual pattern that reflects the
man's soul's return to his Dreaming territory. Usually
there are stories and songs associated with his journey
which are all related to the motifs in the sand. The man's

bones (crushed now, and stored in a hollow log after having been exhumed) are often placed in a shady place nearby, as if to observe the spirit's final return to the *alcheringa*. What occurs next is that the clan members recreate various song elements in dance and mime. The men sit about in the *djel* and await their turn to be ceremonially 'washed' by the *anmari*. He asks them individually to step inside a 'well' fashioned from the sand where he proceeds to pour water over them. Thus they are cleansed and later smeared with red ochre as a sign of being reborn in the deceased's Dreaming territory, along with his soul. In an act of mimicry each man is able to partake of the spirit's journey back to its source in the *alcheringa*. It is an important moment for everyone since the spiritual map at their feet has guided them past the clashing rocks of reality into a more luminous realm.

Probably I have taken leave of my senses in my naïve willingness to wander among sage patterns on the ground. But is this not the sole purpose of living? Remember, pressing back the infinite can only be done by acknowledging one's *own* increase. In contrast, we fritter away our primal cause in consequences, hoping to allay the demands of unity by engaging in spurious acts of little substance. We are addicted to exploring the realm of the possible rather than addressing what might be immortal in ourselves. Clearly, this is why the Yolngu fashion these *djel* in the sand. They know that at some point in their lives (or in death) they must fashion for themselves a metaphysical map to remind them of where they are going. Our inability to focus attention on the existence of a transcendent world is at the root of the grave environmental predicament we find ourselves in today. Because of our failure to recognise that there is *another* life which we are entitled to live if we so wish, we have condemned ourselves to waging a war of attrition against the physical world itself. The image of one small man atop his mighty earthmover, at the bottom of an open-cut mine, removing ore-bearing earth from its place of repose reflects the true condition of our hearts. Together we inhabit the *malbowges* of hell among the incontinent, a place removed from every glimmer of light. We want to shift things, rearrange, reassemble. With science as our helpmate we have extended our power to *reconstruct* nature in our own image. The trouble is the image we have of ourselves is governed by a relentless vision of progress that has *no* end to which we are forced to adhere. Instead of living in accordance with the cyclic principles of the laws of nature and the idea of eternal return and renewal, we have chosen to embark upon a voyage towards attaining a perfect material condition. This beacon flashes on every illusory headland, drawing us towards the rocks. In so doing, we have become victims of a continuing need to undergo change, rather than simply to be.

Out here in the wild, this is the law. Things *are*, whether it is a spoonbill foraging in the shallows or a darter dancing across a bridge of lotus leaves floating on the water. Whatever adaptation goes on—and it does, with infinite slowness—these adjustments are made in response to, not in spite of, the environment because nature believes in itself. Not in thinking terms as we know it, but in *living* terms. Each tree, each shrub, every boulder and cliff face lives its own life, though without the burden of self-consciousness. In the words of the Chhandogya Upanishad, 'Earth, sky, heaven, water, mountain, men, gods, meditate. The greatness of the great comes from

meditation'. This is what we find so difficult to understand: there is an integrity to all life that transcends the
criteria we place upon it in terms of psychological and
physiological processes. By dismissing the tree that thinks
photosynthetically we are drawing a distinction between
ourselves and all other forms of life.

Was this not the true crime of Adam which caused his
exile? Separating himself from nature through knowledge?
My nomad friends seem to think so. They maintain that
people like us, those who surround themselves with the
paraphernalia of modern existence, cannot truly know nature except in a quantitative sense. Formulating an equation has become our substitute for reverence or the
utterance of a prayer. We look to the pontifical statements
of experts, political and scientific, to lull us into a false
state of security, instead of listening to the entreaties of
nature. We are so wedded to the passage of time that we
have marginalised the eternal in our pursuit of the purely
temporal. In so doing, we are unable to respond to nature,
to the land we inhabit, because we have lost the capacity to
deify it by way of myth and story. The Rainbow Snake no
longer slithers up river as it did during the *alcheringa*, cre-
ating mountain ranges and watercourses in its wake. Nor
are the Mimi allowed to preserve the bond between soil
and soul for people such as ourselves. When Henry Tho-
reau asked us to grow wild according to our nature, like
the brakes and sedges, he was alerting us to the dangers of
becoming too civilised, too dependent upon material well-
being in order to survive.

Dear friend, I realise now why I have been reluctant to
return to the world we both know. Coming to grips with
the wild state has been a long and salutary process. Journeying through the bush has taught me, firstly, how to

embrace *rawness*. You see, I had to learn to recognise the *genius loci*, or guardian spirit, that secretly watches over every tree, every creek and every hill. By doing so I have been able to discover for myself how important it is to placate this spirit before embarking upon any act of exploitation. It is this knowledge that we moderns have forgotten how to use. Is it any wonder, then, that until recently when we heard of a factory discharging its poisonous effluent into a river system that we reacted with only mild indifference? For we have been too much enamoured by what the factory has produced to pay attention to the death of life in that river. We have weighed nature and found it wanting, preferring the mean product of industry to the beneficence of nature's *gift*.

Indeed, sitting here in a sand sculpture waiting to be ceremonially washed, makes me conscious of the task that confronts us all. Contemporary materialism is a savage side-show, a wilful performance by people who are out of kilter with nature. All thirst for limpidity has been sated by a brew more potent than any sorcerer might concoct. It is as if we have become blinded by our own capacity for self-destruction. Like moths we're forever attacking the luminosity that made us, until we finally destroy ourselves. Nature and the physical environment constitutes this light, however much we might wish to deny it. The eternal flame which we confine to war memorials as a symbol of sacrifice is in danger of guttering. Why? Because we have lost the sensibility which in the past bound us to all that is mysterious in nature. The Mimi, those shy silhouettes from the realm of faerie, have been exiled to the crevasses from whence they came. Few people today know how gently to blow on the palm of their hand and invoke the presence of these stick people any more. This is because few today will allow themselves the joy of embracing the wildness that once inhabited their own souls.

How I wish I could convince you that to join me among the sand ridges of this *djel* would bind us both to a new perception of our individual destiny, and of reality itself. What are we, after all, if not a momentary balance between a multitude of hidden actions that are not specifically human? In a wild state these actions manifest themselves most acutely, paving the way for a new intimacy between ourselves and nature which can only be equated with the bliss of the hermit. He alone holds the secret to such a communion, since his very being is identified with the desert (Latin: *eremita*, meaning wilderness or desert). I therefore implore you—come, join me here in the bush where the true sages are men who are immune from secular knowledge as we know it. Such men are known as *mekigars*, or men of high degree. Their acute level of insight into matters of the *alcheringa* have made them ideal exemplars for people such as ourselves.

The truth is, dear friend, you and I are tarred with the same brush. We each represent aspects of our mutual dilemma. On the one hand, I uphold a break with our present materialist condition where all thought is made subservient to the needs of producing in excess of what we require. You, on the other hand, ask me to dismiss my yearning to return to some sort of wild state whereby the mind is made subservient to the imperatives of survival. Clearly, each position is extreme. Implicit in both arguments is the desire to transform the human predicament. As human beings we carry on two legs all possible varieties of pain and the utmost sensual pleasure. Yet we also carry our death as if it were a precious secret, a hidden treasure, and a guarantee of the end of things.

The real question is whether we wish to die in the conflagration caused by a holocaust of our own making, or in the proximity of the *alcheringa* ancestors who linger among the symbolic patterns of the *djel*, invisible spirits all of them, whose eternality is capable of quivering in our very essence, allowing us to hear what Pasternak called an 'inner music'—that is, the irresistible power of unarmed truth.

To give up much of what we have acquired in the name of progress is the greatest challenge facing us today. I have no solution to this problem, nor do I wish to impose one. All I know is that our addiction to the material condition is leading us farther from the realm of wildness because we have chosen to destroy it. The whale sickens in a sea of stricken algae. Ferns wither in a sunlight previously kept out by a canopy of branches overhead. All about us is evidence of a devastation that we seem to be willing upon ourselves. Remember the Kadimakara, those Sky Heroes who could not stop eating their own habitat? In the end they ate the trees that provided them with a ladder back to their source. They consumed what linked them to the eternal. Is this not what we are doing when we abuse the wildness within us?

To many, these tribesmen may appear to be little more than primitives. Their pantheism is considered to be the remnant of a rudimentary system of belief. In contrast, we moderns are encouraged to think we have 'progressed', that we have assumed some refinement of sensibility which sets us apart. Yet I know of no criteria by which one can make such a judgement. The quality in a man, surely, can be judged by the respect he shows for his environment. When he desecrates that, then we may be sure he has lost all feeling for reverence. As Uncle Noah, a Juki gypsy, once remarked, '. . . our loyalty is not to the great causes which are celebrated in the kingdoms and states of our age. We owe a debt only to Life, herself, our great benefactress, for her works cannot be contained and defined away by bearers of causes'. My friends would readily concur with Uncle Noah. Sitting in a sand sculpture with water coursing down their limbs is their way of acknowledging that debt, I'm sure.

In your letter you asked me whether I will ever return. Of course! Though I hope in possession of a more rigorous disdain for contemporary values. The task lying before us is one of breaking the vicious circle that encloses us in its capsule of comfort. Like Faust, every man longs to embrace and experience and express everything in the world. It is the modern dilemma not to define any limits. For my friends the limits they impose upon themselves are defined by the Dreaming, the other-worldly home of the ancestors. We must relearn how to impose these same limits upon ourselves. Instead of remaining in league with our own perils, the chimerical allure of *newness*, we must begin by renewing our relationship with what is eternal. Indeed, an exclusive penchant for what is new and merely new points to a degeneration of the critical faculty itself, for nothing is quite so easy as to gauge the 'novelty' of anything.

Living in a wild state implies a recognition that something coeval exists between man and nature, a correspondence. Emanuel Swedenborg was sure of this when he said:

> I have been instructed from heaven, that the most ancient natives of our earth, who were celestial men, thought from correspondences themselves, and that the natural objects

of the world, which they had before their eyes, served them as mediums for such contemplations; and that, as being of such character, they enjoyed consociation with the angels, and held conversation with them, heaven was conjoined to the world.

My nomad friends understand this to mean a parley between themselves and the Mimi, an inner dialogue with the numinous in nature. Could this be a language we have forgotten in our haste to deliver ourselves from the constraints that we believe exist in the wild state?

According to one wise man I know, the syntax of this language is the *symbolic vision*, or the ability to transmute our mode of perception so the perceiver and that which is perceived are metamorphosed by the spontaneity of the imagination. How else can a man borrow from the visible world those forces which help him to identify with the feeling of matter itself, except by using his imaginative faculty? Rocks, air, water, vegetable matter—all these have elemental properties which are buried in our being as well. Living in a wild state implies a recognition that such properties are the true currency of exchange between ourselves and the *alcheringa*.

All I ask, dear friend, is for you to join me out here, if only in spirit. The act of sitting in a *djel* is a symbolic act of rebirth for both of us. To think the sand beneath our feet embodies every constituent that makes up ourselves! What is nearest to us, therefore, allows us to conduct internal exchanges which are at the furthest point from monetary values. What is essential to our nature derives its sustenance from a condition that is without value from an economic viewpoint, yet nevertheless exhorts us to respect it as priceless. This, surely, is why we entered the *djel* in the first place—to begin the process of *rap-*

prochement between ourselves and all that we find inimical in nature. In the end, the smile of a rock python becomes an expression of our contumacy. After all, do we not both share the same terrestial tent, and the same celestial pavilion?

Your friend

EPILOGUE

Is it possible to allow a state of wildness to enter our consciousness again? This is the question all of us individually must ask if we are to arrive at any conclusion. It is certain that no government can legislate such a condition into existence, even if it had the power to do so. The wild state cannot be conceptualised, only seen and felt. A kangaroo, raising its head to observe you manifests all the symptoms of wildness when it hesitates. The quivering nose, the motionless stance, the perfection of the animal's silhouette against the setting sun—these are what make wildness such a moving experience for us all. No man can gaze upon one of nature's creatures in the open and not feel the deep stirring of a bond between himself and the animal, tenuous perhaps, but nevertheless profoundly satisfying. At this moment he has encountered one of the great paradigms of life, what the poet St John Perse called 'the full shower of the health-giving god'.

These letters may serve to highlight one small aspect of the challenge we face as we enter the twenty-first century: how to shrug off the weight of accumulated *constraints* we have imposed upon ourselves in our quest for greater sophistication. The time has come, perhaps, to say 'no' to the relentless pursuit of modernity for its own sake, knowing as we do how fragmented our sensibility has become in the process. The fact is that at every moment we exist within a consciousness larger and more general than all our attempts to comprehend it. We need to allow this consciousness, which is none other than the incipient processes of nature itself, more freedom of expression within the deeper recesses of our being. If the kangaroo can do it, why can't we?

The truth is I have travelled vast distances in pursuit of this knowledge. In the old days if a man wished to deepen his understanding of himself and the world, he would travel afar to find a teacher at whose feet he might sit and learn. The great Arab theologian and mystic, Ibn Arabi, travelled from Spain through North Africa to Damascus and beyond to become a sage. He encountered his *khidr* (celestial guide) in the form of a young woman, Nizam, who became for him the 'Eye of the Sun and of Beauty' who later inspired some of his finest mystical poems. Dante accompanied Virgil and later Beatrice in his journey through Hell and Heaven. The Greek writer Nikos Kazantzakis acknowledged Zorba as his guide. It follows that each man must seek out his *khidr* in his own way, wherever and however the *khidr* might choose to reveal himself, even if it means meeting with simple men of the steppes or the forest.

The wild state, I now know, is a condition of the heart. Some might regard it as an aspect of humility; others naïveté. However we regard it we must treat it as a priceless ornament, one that we allow to regale all our actions and so enhance their splendour. My nomad friends struggle with the great metaphors of existence in the same way that we do. Their answers, though filled with the accumulated poetry of countless generations, are often more pristine than our own carefully reasoned formulations. Though the Black Hole or the Big Bang theory may satisfy some as to the origins of the universe, I know my friends would find such scientific rationalism discomforting. For it would lack noesis—that is, a complete moral and metaphysical perception to give it substance. They do not see why we moderns should *separate* our thought into sacred and secular compartments. To them unity stands for something more durable than our mind babbling to itself, however beautiful it might sound.

I do not advocate a return to the life of our Paleolithic forebears. This would be impractical and impossible given the world we live in today. Nor do I ask that we reject the great gifts bestowed upon us under the mantle of progress. But I do suggest we reassess the uncritical way in which we allow ourselves to become prisoners within the kraal of modernism. The nemesis that dogs our footsteps is not chaos but the illusion of well-being that our insatiable desire for gadgetry imposes. We have become slaves to our *things,* to our self-creations, rather than to Creation itself. We have immersed ourselves in change for change's sake, rather than explore what Paul Valéry called the 'sweet ease of the sun in a crystal universe'. He meant, I suspect, the pure lucidity of being that comes about when our ideas transform ordinary reality—that is, sensible forms—into theophanic vision. This, and this alone, is the one thing capable of helping us to break the spell which we have allowed to be cast over our intellects by the physical sciences for so long. The *meta*-physical sciences have yet to impose their authority upon our minds and hearts once more, thus releasing us from the long sleep of realism to which we have succumbed.

Is this too much to ask of ourselves? Traditional peoples live within their own poem even if we sometimes lack the ability to translate their lives into a language that we understand. My nomad friends taught me to respect their existence for what it is: simple, uncluttered, wild. It may not produce great works of art or scientific discoveries of note, but it does have the power to explore the most mysterious realm of all—that of the interworld. Let us give praise, then, for their discovery of what is purely imaginary within ourselves: the wild spirit of nature that lies in the fathomless gaze of all animals when they acknowledge *us* as being at one with them.

GLOSSARY

Alcheringa: *A Central Australian Aboriginal word for the metaphysical concept of the Dreaming. The mythical time when the ancestors were supposed to have lived.*

Axis mundi: *The vertical axis which represents the metaphysical locus of the world. Passing through the horizontal plane, it reflects the complete point of harmonization of all the elements making up that particular state of being.*

Baraka: *An Arabic word meaning spiritual influence or blessing. A Sufi holy man may bestow it on a disciple as a reward for his piety.*

Birrimbirr: *A soul bird which departs the body after death and is said to return to the person's country where it enters the reservoir of Spirit.*

Conjunctio: *Derived from alchemy,* conjunctio *is the 'chymical marriage' allegorizing the ritual cohabitation of Sol and Luna (sun and moon). From this union the hermaphrodite Mercurius evolved as a symbol of fully rounded perfection.*

Dhikr: *The practice of remembrance of God through repetition of His name in Sufi ritual.*

Dilly bag: *A small grass bag used to carry ochre or sacred objects.*

Djang: *(Arnhem Land of Northern Australia) The spiritual power inherent in a place linked to the exploits of Sky Heroes from the Dreaming.*

Djel: *A sand sculpture associated with mortuary rites in northern Australia.*

Duat: *The Egyptian Underworld through which souls must pass after death.*

Gravitas: *Popular among Stoics, it represented a philosophic or spiritual presence, a dignity.*

Kurunba: *(Walbiri tribe of Central Australia) Spiritual essence associated with sacred places, similar to* djang.

Likan: *The meeting point between two relativities, the terrestrial and the supernal. It also signifies an elevated condition whereby a person transcends his ordinary mode of existence.*

Maraiin: *A similar concept to* djang *or* kurunba *implying sanctity, sacred, the embodiment of Spirit in a place or ritual object.*

Mekigar: *Tribal hierophant, medicine man, and spiritual exemplar. The responsibilities for cultural continuity were his principal concern.*

Mevlana: *A name given to Jalaluddin Rumi, the thirteenth-century Persian poet from Konya in Turkey. He wrote the* Mathnawi *and the* Divan of Shems of Tabriz.

Mokuy: *The darker, chthonic aspect of the soul. The life-force. The* mokuy *spirit must be released from the body at death in order to return to the clan territory where all* mokuy *spirits live.*

Orafä: *A Persian or Shiite word denoting a sage, philosopher, mystic, or one with superior spiritual insight.*

Paraunda: *Spiritual power in place, similar to* djang.

Pîr: *A Sufi spiritual master or guide.*

Primordial: *The first moment, usually associated with world creation. It* *does, however, imply time-spanning as in the eternally present nature of the Dreaming.*

Urbicus: *Latin. Pertaining to the city, or city life.*

Zogo le: *A man of High Degree, or spiritual power among the Torres Strait Islanders, similar to a* mekigar.

SELECTED BIBLIOGRAPHY

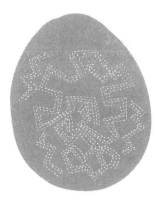

Barr, James. 'Of Metaphysics and Polynesian Navigation' *Avaloka* Vol. III, Nos. 1 & 2, 1989.

Corbin, Henry. *Avicenna and the Visionary Recital*, trans. William R. Trask, Spring Publications, 1980.

———. *Creative Imagination in the Sufism of Ibn Arabi*, trans. Ralph Manheim, Bollingen Books, 1969.

Cowan, James. *Mysteries of the Dreaming*, Prism Books, 1989.

Montesquieu, Charles. *The Persian Letters*, trans. J. Robert Loy, Meridian Books, 1961.

Morphy, Howard. *Journey to the Crocodile's Nest*, Australian Institute of Aboriginal Studies, Canberra, Australia, 1984.

Neidjie, Bill. *Kakadu Man*, Resources Managers, Darwin, Australia, 1986.

Nerval, Gerard de. *Selected Writings*, trans. Geoffrey Wagner, Panther Books, London, 1973.

Perse, St. John. *Collected Poems*, trans. Louise Varèse, Bollingen Books, 1983.

Rilke, Rainer Maria. *Duino Elegies,* trans. J. B. Leishman and Stephen Spender, W. W. Norton, 1963.

Rimbaud, Arthur. *A Season in Hell,* trans. Louise Varèse, New Directions, 1945.

Spencer & Gillen. *Native Tribes of Central Australia,* Macmillan, 1898.

Swedenborg, Emanuel. *Heaven and Hell,* Swedenborg Society, 1958.

Valéry, Paul. *Monsieur Teste,* trans. Jackson Mathews, Princeton University Press, 1983.

A NOTE
ABOUT THE AUTHOR

James G. Cowan is a distinguished author and poet. He has spent much of his life exploring the world of traditional peoples such as the Berbers of Morocco, the Tuareg of the Central Sahara, and the Australian Aborigines. He spent a decade living and travelling in Europe and North America, and then returned to his home in Australia, where he embarked on a series of books that explored the agricultural peoples of early Australia. These books were followed by others dealing with Aboriginal metaphysics and cosmology. James Cowan has also written fiction, contributed articles to magazines, given lectures, and made documentaries for Australian television. He lives in Sydney, where in his spare time he breeds Arabian horses.

OTHER
BELL TOWER BOOKS

*The pure sound
of the bell
summons us
into the present moment.
The timeless ring of truth
is expressed in
many different voices,
each one magnifying
and illuminating
the sacred.
The clarity of its song
resonates within us
and calls us away
from those things
which often distract us—
that which was,
that which might be—
to That Which Is.*

BEING HOME
A Book of Meditations
by Gunilla Norris
Photographs by Greta D. Sibley
An exquisite modern book of hours,
   a celebration of mindfulness in
   everyday activities.
Hardcover 0-517-58159-0

NOURISHING WISDOM
A New Understanding of Eating
by Marc David
A practical way out of dietary
   confusion, a book that reveals
   how our attitude to food reflects
   our attitude to life.
Hardcover 0-517-57636-8

SANCTUARIES
*A Guide to Lodgings in
   Monasteries, Abbeys, and Retreats
   of the United States: The Northeast*
by Jack and Marcia Kelly
The first in a series of regional
   guides for those in search of
   renewal and a little peace.
Softcover 0-517-57727-5

GRACE UNFOLDING
*Psychotherapy in the Spirit of the
Tao-te ching*
by Greg Johanson and Ron Kurtz
The interaction of client and
therapist illuminated through the
gentle power and wisdom of Lao
Tzu's ancient Chinese classic.
Hardcover 0-517-58449-2

SELF-RELIANCE
*The Wisdom of Ralph Waldo Emerson
as Inspiration for Daily Living*
Selected and with an introduction
by Richard Whelan
A distillation of Emerson's essential
spiritual writings for contemporary
readers.
Softcover 0-517-58512-X

COMPASSION IN ACTION
Setting Out on the Path of Service
by Ram Dass and Mirabai Bush
Heartfelt encouragement and advice
for those ready to commit time
and energy to relieving suffering
in the world.
Softcover 0-517-57635-X

SILENCE, SIMPLICITY, AND
SOLITUDE
A Guide for Spiritual Retreat
by David A. Cooper
This classic guide to meditation and
other traditional spiritual
practices will be required reading
for anyone contemplating a
retreat.
Hardcover 0-517-58620-7